SOLO

THE MESSAGE: SOLO
WOMEN'S DEVOTIONAL

SOLO

NavPress is the publishing ministry of The Navigators, an international Christian organization and leader in personal spiritual development. NavPress is committed to helping people grow spiritually and enjoy lives of meaning and hope through personal and group resources that are biblically rooted, culturally relevant, and highly practical.

For a free catalog go to www.NavPress.com
or call 1.800.366.7788 in the United States or 1.800.839.4769 in Canada.

ISBN-13: 978-1-61291-454-1

Some of the anecdotal illustrations in this book are true to life and are included with the permission of the persons involved. All other illustrations are composites of real situations, and any resemblance to people living or dead is coincidental.

All Scripture quotations in this publication are taken from *THE MESSAGE* (msg), copyright © 1993, 1994, 1995, 1996, 2000, 2001, 2002, used by permission of NavPress Publishing Group.

Devotional text by Michelle Hindman.

Published in association with the literary agency of Alive Communications, Inc., 7680 Goddard Street, Suite 200, Colorado Springs, CO 80920, www.alivecommunications.com.

Printed in the United States of America

1 2 3 4 5 6 7 8 / 19 18 17 16 15 14

INTRODUCTION TO *SOLO*

The devotional you hold is unique. It isn't designed to teach you to study the Bible but rather to develop a conversation between you and God. The devotions found in *Solo* are based on the classical method of *lectio divina*: reading, thinking, praying, and living Scripture with the intention of inviting an infinite, omniscient God into your life — as it is, no gloss, no veneer. Lectio divina is more Bible basking than Bible study, as it teaches you to absorb and meditate on Scripture, converse with God openly, and live out what has become a part of you: his Word.

But it's not easy. Lectio divina takes practice, and lots of it. You will have to learn to be quiet, to silence the voices of responsibility, self, family, and even religion in order to hear what God has to say to you. Try not to view the elements of lectio divina as steps to be checked off your to-do list. Instead, allow them to meld together in the intentional process of listening to God, of focusing on him and learning what he would have from you and for you, his beloved. Don't worry if no lightning strikes or brilliant revelations come. Sometimes devotion means just sitting in the presence of God.

We know the four elements of lectio divina as Read, Think, Pray, and Live. Each element has a purpose, but don't be surprised if they overlap and weave into each other. Remember as you dive into this devotional that lectio divina is about wholeness: whole practice, whole Bible, whole God.

Read. Thoughtfully, leisurely, faithfully — read the epic love story that is the Bible. Yes, love story. The Bible is the chronicle of God's love for his people from the darkness before Eden to eternity with him in heaven. You are in it, I am in it, and, most important, God is in it. Here you will meet him face-to-face.

Eugene Peterson called the Bible "a book that reads us even as we read it." That's an uncommon sort of book, and it requires an uncommon sort of read. Knowing facts about God doesn't change your relationship with him, so take the time to splash around in the Word, to absorb it, to discover what God has to say to you each day.

In each *Solo* devotion, you will find a Scripture passage but also a reference to an expanded passage. I encourage you to read them both, slowly, attentively, and repeatedly. As Peterson said, "The Bible is given to us in the first place simply to invite us to make ourselves at home in the world of God . . . and become familiar with the way God speaks and the ways in which we answer him with our lives." No Scripture passage exists in a vacuum. Whenever you can, take the time to stretch beyond the passage put before you to understand the larger context in which it is found. The more you read, the more you will understand about yourself and this God who created you.

Think. Each subtle, significant, powerful word of Scripture is meant for you. One word may speak today and another tomorrow, but God sent each of them straight into your life. So listen. Go into your reading with a clean slate. Don't bring what you think you need to hear, what others have said, or what you've been taught about a particular passage. Don't bring fear that you'll misinterpret the text. This is about what God has to say to you.

Our lives are full of static. Whether it's our to-do lists, our emotions, or just plain noise, it can be hard to sift out God's voice from all the racket. By meditating on each word, by turning it over and over in your mind, you will discover that as God himself is infinitely complex, so his thoughts have subtle meaning beyond the rote. The more you think about what you read, the more familiar you will become with his voice.

Pray. God yearns to converse with you. And he wants far more than just "thanks for this, can I please have that" prayer. Respond to him in dialogue. That means it's as much about listening as it is about speaking. Open your ears and your heart to hear his voice. Sing praises or laments; write your thoughts in a journal; dance or prostrate yourself before him. Pray.

Maybe God has challenged you. Tell him how you feel, but always remember that what he asks, he asks for your good. He is loving and merciful, not manipulative and harsh. If you come across something in your reading that you don't understand, tell him about it. Ask him about it. Fill your prayers with Scripture. Using the words you have read helps you ensure that your prayers line up with God's Word and intention for your life.

It's easy for us in our culture of doing to want to skim over this part. Don't. Even if you are quiet and God is quiet, you are learning to communicate with him.

Live. You can read, think, and pray all day, but unless you live in God's Word as well, you miss the point. The Bible says, "Isn't it obvious that God-talk without God-acts is outrageous nonsense?" (James 2:17). If you have taken God's Word to heart and truly made it part of you, it will by its very nature change you. And when it does, you will find yourself called to act. There will come a time when God takes you to the end of yourself then asks you to go further. He wants you to put yourself at his disposal, to go and do what he asks, even the impossible. When that time comes, you will need the Word he has seared on your heart to give you comfort and strength. This is the "more and better life than they ever dreamed of " of which Jesus spoke (John 10:10).

ONE THING ONLY

LUKE 10:38-42

38-40 As they continued their travel, Jesus entered a village. A woman by the name of Martha welcomed him and made him feel quite at home. She had a sister, Mary, who sat before the Master, hanging on every word he said. But Martha was pulled away by all she had to do in the kitchen. Later, she stepped in, interrupting them. "Master, don't you care that my sister has abandoned the kitchen to me? Tell her to lend me a hand."

41-42 The Master said, "Martha, dear Martha, you're fussing far too much and getting yourself worked up over nothing. One thing only is essential, and Mary has chosen it — it's the main course, and won't be taken from her."

READ

Read this passage aloud slowly. What sights, sounds, and emotions surface? Where would you be in the story?

THINK

Just before this passage in Luke, Christ told the parable of the Good Samaritan. Martha's eagerness to make Christ at home could portray her as a "good" woman, ready to leap into action. Why then does Jesus chide Martha and say Mary's choice is lasting? What is her choice? Is it your presence or your performance God values? Can a sense of obligation become confused with our identity? What if, in your eagerness to *accomplish*, you have neglected relationship with God and others? What if you are missing "the main course"?

PRAY

Confess the clutter. Tell God what tasks tire you. Be honest if you feel abandoned to an overwhelming job by those who seem to sit still. Reveal to God what pulls you away from listening. Then consider God's ability compared to your own. Praise him for requiring nothing but your love, and ask for the ability to discern between necessary work and "fussing." Thank him for offering us good things that last rather than toil that wears us down.

LIVE

While our eagerness to be good workers is not wrong, Christ's message is clear: Completed lists and flawless events are not the lasting stuff of eternity. He claims only one thing is essential. Today, make room in your life for that one thing: sitting at the feet of Jesus.

1

• even when physical rest isn't an option; rest for my mind + focus on hanging on every word from Jesus.

ABSOLUTELY CONVINCED

ROMANS 8:31-39

31-39 So, what do you think? With God on our side like this, how can we lose? If God didn't hesitate to put everything on the line for us, embracing our condition and exposing himself to the worst by sending his own Son, is there anything else he wouldn't gladly and freely do for us? And who would dare tangle with God by messing with one of God's chosen? Who would dare even to point a finger? The One who died for us — who was raised to life for us! — is in the presence of God at this very moment sticking up for us. Do you think anyone is going to be able to drive a wedge between us and Christ's love for us? There is no way! Not trouble, not hard times, not hatred, not hunger, not homelessness, not bullying threats, not backstabbing, not even the worst sins listed in Scripture:

> They kill us in cold blood because they hate you.
> We're sitting ducks; they pick us off one by one.

None of this fazes us because Jesus loves us. I'm absolutely convinced that nothing — nothing living or dead, angelic or demonic, today or tomorrow, high or low, thinkable or unthinkable — absolutely *nothing* can get between us and God's love because of the way that Jesus our Master has embraced us.

READ

Read this passage aloud with appropriate energy. Imagine you are encouraging a dear friend at a critical moment and then read it again.

THINK

We are so often defined by our wounds and by the circumstances that we find ourselves in, crushed by our failures or brought too high by our fleeting successes. We assume these things swallow us up and put us far from God's sight. But that is not the case "because of the way that Jesus our Master has embraced us." Ask yourself each of Paul's many questions honestly before you soak in the answers he provides.

PRAY

God is inconceivably *big* and *beyond* and yet beckoning to our small selves. Ponder the Maker's many qualities, then allow yourself to melt in the truth that *he* is "sticking up for us" and "on our side" as you pour out your heart in prayer.

LIVE

What is the "unthinkable" today that you assume stands between you and God? Name it and then praise him for the victory he has already secured for you.

Short temper & annoyance w misbehavior from my kids.

Rom 8:5-6 "Those who live according to the flesh have their minds set on what the flesh desires; but those who live in accordance w the Spirit have their minds set on what the Spirit desires"

2

FIXED AND FIT TOGETHER

COLOSSIANS 1:15-20

15-18 We look at this Son and see the God who cannot be seen. We look at this Son and see God's original purpose in everything created. For everything, absolutely everything, above and below, visible and invisible, rank after rank after rank of angels — *everything* got started in him and finds its purpose in him. He was there before any of it came into existence and holds it all together right up to this moment. And when it comes to the church, he organizes and holds it together, like a head does a body.

18-20 He was supreme in the beginning and — leading the resurrection parade — he is supreme in the end. From beginning to end he's there, towering far above everything, everyone. So spacious is he, so roomy, that everything of God finds its proper place in him without crowding. Not only that, but all the broken and dislocated pieces of the universe — people and things, animals and atoms — get properly fixed and fit together in vibrant harmonies, all because of his death, his blood that poured down from the cross.

READ

Read the passage aloud slowly. Pause. What words, phrases, and ideas stand out? What stops you in your tracks?

THINK

Why does Paul emphasize Christ's place in the universe? Ancient believers sometimes had trouble accepting the full impact of Christ's godhood — and maybe so do you. Do you tend to separate "big" God — who is out there, somewhere — from the person of Jesus who walked the earth, who hung on the cross for your sins? The incredibly powerful One who shaped the stars and breathed your atoms into being also came down to wash his disciples' dusty feet — and yours. What does the power of Christ mean for your relationship with him?

PRAY

Repent of any small view you might have of Christ's power. Praise the Lord for his incredible and multifaceted power. Request to be aware of his ability and a part of that all-encompassing harmony.

LIVE

If Christ brings harmony and peace and meaning, he can bring those things into your life today if you put him in his proper place, "towering far above everything, everyone." Today, make a point of pausing to praise him for who he truly is, even in your crazy world.

✳ Baby girl- God already knows her story & he loves her more than anyone on this earth ever could. I will wait in expectation still, but also trust & have peace in knowing her life isn't hanging in the balance— it is perfectly planned out already.

3

LOVE DOES

1 CORINTHIANS 13:3-7

3-7 If I give everything I own to the poor and even go to the stake to be burned as a martyr, but I don't love, I've gotten nowhere. So, no matter what I say, what I believe, and what I do, I'm bankrupt without love.

Love never gives up.
Love cares more for others than for self.
Love doesn't want what it doesn't have.
Love doesn't strut,
Doesn't have a swelled head,
Doesn't force itself on others,
Isn't always "me first,"
Doesn't fly off the handle,
Doesn't keep score of the sins of others,
Doesn't revel when others grovel,
Takes pleasure in the flowering of truth,
Puts up with anything,
Trusts God always,
Always looks for the best,
Never looks back,
But keeps going to the end.

READ

Read this famous passage, as much as possible, without preconceptions. Savor the words and the images. Read it several times, pausing after each phrase.

THINK

As the author says, good actions without love are worthless. Likewise, relationships without love — real, on-the-ground love — are simply a show. Take some time to journal about how this definition of love compares and contrasts to a relationship you have as wife, mother, sister, or daughter.

_____

_____

_____

PRAY

Without God, true love is impossible. Ask God to forgive your selfish and backward interpretations of love and to show you with his Spirit what it means to truly love those in your life as he loves you. Ask for new eyes and new motivation to be selfless and others-focused. Thank him for not leaving you to reach this standard on your own.

LIVE

No matter how much our earthly relationships fail to reflect this, remember that God has fulfilled this definition of love toward you perfectly — every word. Let that be your fuel when you feel discouraged today. Infinite love is offered you and is running through you.

STRENGTH! COURAGE!

JOSHUA 1:1-9

1-9 After the death of Moses the servant of GOD, GOD spoke to Joshua, Moses'
assistant:

"Moses my servant is dead. Get going. Cross this Jordan River, you and
all the people. Cross to the country I'm giving to the People of Israel. I'm
giving you every square inch of the land you set your foot on — just as I
promised Moses. From the wilderness and this Lebanon east to the Great
River, the Euphrates River — all the Hittite country — and then west to
the Great Sea. It's all yours. All your life, no one will be able to hold out
against you. In the same way I was with Moses, I'll be with you. I won't
give up on you; I won't leave you. Strength! Courage! You are going to
lead this people to inherit the land that I promised to give their ances-
tors. Give it everything you have, heart and soul! Make sure you carry out
The Revelation that Moses commanded you, every bit of it. Don't get off
track, either left or right, so as to make sure you get to where you're going.
And don't for a minute let this Book of The Revelation be out of mind.
Ponder and meditate on it day and night, making sure you practice everything written in it. Then you'll get where you're going; then you'll succeed.
Haven't I commanded you? Strength! Courage! Don't be timid; don't get
discouraged. God, your God, is with you every step you take."

READ

Read the passage once through. Imagine the setting: You and all of wandering Israel are before the Jordan River. Imagine yourself in Joshua's position: Your mentor has just passed away and his big task has passed to you. Read the passage again.

THINK

What do you think God is intending to convey to Joshua? God is relational; the Lord does not simply issue commands without purpose. How do you think Joshua might have felt upon the loss of his mentor and the gain of huge responsibility? How does God seem to anticipate and respond to those emotions? Why does God tell Joshua to take on such a large task when Joshua is such a green hand? What is Joshua's "task" — what is he told to do? *Do what he has been told to do & stay focused on God - not to the (R) or the (L)*

PRAY

God's commandments and challenges go hand in hand with his abundance and blessing. Confess to God the fears you have about the tasks you have been given. Be honest about your insecurities. Then, thank him in trust for the abundance of blessings that he has prepared for you, just beyond the river. Request strength and courage. *& wisdom!*

LIVE

God tells Joshua firmly, "I won't give up on you; I won't leave you." Regardless of the tasks handed down to you today, take the next steps forward, trusting these promises of God to you.

SIMPLE SURRENDER

ROMANS 12:1-2

1-2 So here's what I want you to do, God helping you: Take your everyday, ordinary life — your sleeping, eating, going-to-work, and walking-around life — and place it before God as an offering. Embracing what God does for you is the best thing you can do for him. Don't become so well-adjusted to your culture that you fit into it without even thinking. Instead, fix your attention on God. You'll be changed from the inside out. Readily recognize what he wants from you, and quickly respond to it. Unlike the culture around you, always dragging you down to its level of immaturity, God brings the best out of you, develops well-formed maturity in you.

READ

As you read, contemplate the action and motivation of this passage. Read it again.

THINK

You may think about "plac[ing] [your life] before God as an offering" to Jesus in dramatic terms: upraised hands and a moment of decision. The familiar phrase calls to mind altars and blood, a final act. Would it be easier if Jesus called for merely one moment of sacrifice? What does it mean that he calls not for one moment of death, but for the totality of our lives? What exactly is the call to action that Paul is giving in this passage? What is the promised result and who is responsible for bringing it about?

PRAY

This passage does promise change by setting goals and working hard. God gives growth: Focusing on him gives transformation. Praise God for his unfailing love that covers every action of your day. Consider his power and his promises as you exult in him.

LIVE

Fix your attention on God today. He wants to bring out the best in you in even the "small things."

HOLDING ON FOR DEAR LIFE

PSALM 91:14-16

14-16   "If you'll hold on to me for dear life," says God,
    "I'll get you out of any trouble.
I'll give you the best of care
    if you'll only get to know and trust me.
Call me and I'll answer, be at your side in bad times;
    I'll rescue you, then throw you a party.
I'll give you a long life,
    give you a long drink of salvation!"

READ

Read this passage slowly. Read it again, considering each line by itself.

THINK

Consider all God offers and promises in this passage. What adjectives come to mind? If "extravagant," "generous," maybe even "over-the-top" come to mind, you are on the right track. What are the conditions that God requires we meet before he gives us his presence and celebrates us? Hint: Look for the "ifs."

PRAY

Confess to God what part of his promises you find most difficult to trust. Prayerfully bring to mind the trouble that seems too nagging, too hidden, or too big for God to rescue you from. Admit the obstacles that stop you from clinging to him for dear life. Ask for a new faith in his protection and mercy. Request eyes to see all that he has already done.

LIVE

Those who trust in God will not be let down. Live like you have nothing to lose today and a Rescuer ever "at your side in bad times."

DAY 8

EXPANDED PASSAGE: MATTHEW 6

FREE FOR FLIGHT

MATTHEW 6:25-26

25-26   If you decide for God, living a life of God-worship, it follows that you don't fuss about what's on the table at mealtimes or whether the clothes in your closet are in fashion. There is far more to your life than the food you put in your stomach, more to your outer appearance than the clothes you hang on your body. Look at the birds, free and unfettered, not tied down to a job description, careless in the care of God. And you count far more to him than birds.

READ

Read the passage, and try not to rush past any phrase. Pause. Read the passage again.

THINK

You are probably not worried that a bad harvest will cause your family to starve, like many of Jesus' original listeners. Yet there is still a constant list of things to worry about, a flurry of fussing that seems to be what keeps you from total chaos. Besides the endless list, is there also the added pressure of tying those tasks to your identity? If you don't eat the right food, wear the right clothes, and accomplish things on time, perhaps others will think less of you. Perhaps you are a bad mother or wife or a bad Christian. So much seems so essential, yet that anxiety is the very thing that keeps us from soaring. Consider your own abilities in the scheme of eternity. Consider God's care for the smallest things, and then ask yourself, *Why am I tied to a "job description" when God is the One who provides?*

PRAY

Ponder all of the concrete ways that God has cared for you in the past and on this very day. Confess to God all of the things that weigh on your heart, that seem to give you the idea that *you* are the one controlling your life. Praise God, who is the giver of all good gifts, and ask him to remain in charge of the "essentials," especially the ones that seem too big for you. Invite the Father to teach you of his care — seek to find the ways that you can be "free and unfettered" in the security of his power and love.

LIVE

Write out the things that give you anxiety, whether the specific tasks of the day ahead or the deeper issues that plague your mind. What weighs on you? Release them, one by one, in the knowledge that your Creator cares for you.

8

_____

_____

_____

DAY 9

EXPANDED PASSAGE: EXODUS 14

WATCH GOD WORK

EXODUS 14:10-14

10 As Pharaoh approached, the Israelites looked up and saw them — Egyptians! Coming at them!

11-12 They were totally afraid. They cried out in terror to GOD. They told Moses, "Weren't the cemeteries large enough in Egypt so that you had to take us out here in the wilderness to die? What have you done to us, taking us out of Egypt? Back in Egypt didn't we tell you this would happen? Didn't we tell you, 'Leave us alone here in Egypt — we're better off as slaves in Egypt than as corpses in the wilderness.'"

13 Moses spoke to the people: "Don't be afraid. Stand firm and watch GOD do his work of salvation for you today. Take a good look at the Egyptians today for you're never going to see them again.

14 GOD will fight the battle for you.
And you? You keep your mouths shut!"

READ

Read the passage once through. This is just before the Israelites crossed the Red Sea. Try to imagine the emotions of the Israelites and the motivation of Moses. Read the passage aloud, dramatically.

THINK

Have you ever felt completely out of control in a situation? Though you may not literally have an army of enemies behind you and an ocean in front of you, you can probably relate to the Israelites' feelings. When we feel doomed to fail, it is easy to blame others, or even God, and idealize the place where you *felt* in control — even if that place was bad for your soul. Why did God bring the Israelites out of Egypt? Why did he put them in a situation that seemed dangerous and uncertain? What do you think he wanted his people to learn?

PRAY

Consider and confess your responses in out-of-control situations. Tell God the times when you have felt alone and besieged, and apologize for the people you have blamed (yourself included). Ask God to grant you a greater trust in him so that when the battles come, you are confident in the outcome. Pray for help in acting out your role in tight spaces — that is, simply to shut your mouth and trust the Warrior-King for deliverance.

LIVE

God's agenda is for your good. God's purpose is never dependent on your own strength, ability, or certainty. Live today in faith that he is taking you to greater freedom than you could ever imagine, even when that freedom might seem frightening.

IN TUNE AND IN STEP

COLOSSIANS 3:15-17

15-17   Let the peace of Christ keep you in tune with each other, in step with each other. None of this going off and doing your own thing. And cultivate thankfulness. Let the Word of Christ — the Message — have the run of the house. Give it plenty of room in your lives. Instruct and direct one another using good common sense. And sing, sing your hearts out to God! Let every detail in your lives — words, actions, whatever — be done in the name of the Master, Jesus, thanking God the Father every step of the way.

READ

Read the passage through slowly, giving plenty of consideration to each of the specific commands.

THINK

Consider moments when you have felt completely in tune with someone else. That sense of being known, that easy joy, is precisely the type of relationship God designed us to have. How can we "keep" that when the culture and our own hearts pull against it? How is the peace of Christ related to the Word of Christ? Remember all that you can about Jesus' promises. What specific aspects could and should have the "run of the house"? Why do you think Paul put a commandment to sing right after a commandment to instruct and direct? How is joy significant in this picture?

PRAY

Ask God for a revelation of his peace. Bring your most important relationships before him and consider with the Spirit how "in tune" you are. Where can the "the Message" control your actions more? Approach Jesus and ask not just for the ability to instruct and direct, but to sing your heart out.

LIVE

It is easy to talk about the peace of Christ as an abstract idea or something we wish on others, like a "good day." But it is a powerful reality in the universe, making us right with God and right with one another. Live today as though the peace of Christ is flooding through you into every encounter — because it is.

THE MAKER OF STARS AND GIVER OF STRENGTH

ISAIAH 40:25-31

25-26   Look at the night skies:
      Who do you think made all this?
Who marches this army of stars out each night,
      counts them off, calls each by name
— so magnificent! so powerful! —
      and never overlooks a single one?

27-31   Why would you ever complain, O Jacob,
      or, whine, Israel, saying,
"GOD has lost track of me.
      He doesn't care what happens to me"?
Don't you know anything? Haven't you been listening?
GOD doesn't come and go. God *lasts*.
      He's Creator of all you can see or imagine.
He doesn't get tired out, doesn't pause to catch his breath.
      And he knows *everything*, inside and out.
He energizes those who get tired,
      gives fresh strength to dropouts.
For even young people tire and drop out,
      young folk in their prime stumble and fall.
But those who wait upon GOD get fresh strength.
      They spread their wings and soar like eagles,
They run and don't get tired,
      they walk and don't lag behind.

READ

God is the speaker of the passage. Read the passage remembering that these are God's words directly to his people and his loving words directly to you. Try to visualize the images the passage presents.

THINK

How are you weary and tired today? Is it the exhaustion of a moment or of a whole season? Is it deeper weariness than a night's sleep can fix? Think about how the passage begins and ends. God knows that your weariness sometimes seems as crushing as gravity and as big as the solar system. Perhaps it is hard to even imagine yourself ever being rested or caught up. Do you feel like a "dropout"? He is reminding you today that he effortlessly accounts for all of the stars in the universe and arranges them in beauty. Your exhaustion could not thwart the ability of God. Is there condemnation of the weary ones mentioned in this passage — or something entirely different?

PRAY

Be honest with God about your crushing weariness. Ask the Spirit to help you uncover the sources of that exhaustion. If thinking about your tiredness begins to overwhelm you, stop and remember all the characteristics of God. Praise the Star-maker and Rest-giver — "so magnificent! so powerful!" — and ask for his strength to flood through and supply your weakness.

LIVE

God commands the readers of the passage to look at the stars. As you go out today, look for other signs of his power, might, and beauty in the natural world or simply in the interactions around you. Make it your private covenant to remind yourself that God raises up the weary.

11

MARVELOUSLY MADE

PSALM 139:13-16

13-16   Oh yes, you shaped me first inside, then out;
       you formed me in my mother's womb.
I thank you, High God — you're breathtaking!
       Body and soul, I am marvelously made!
       I worship in adoration — what a creation!
You know me inside and out,
       you know every bone in my body;
You know exactly how I was made, bit by bit,
       how I was sculpted from nothing into something.
Like an open book, you watched me grow from conception to birth;
       all the stages of my life were spread out before you,
The days of my life all prepared
       before I'd even lived one day.

READ

Read the passage with expression. Don't be shy with the exclamation marks — they are there for a reason!

THINK

What was difficult for you about reading this passage? Is this a passage that you are comfortable quoting to others but find difficult applying to yourself? When you consider your life — the way you spend your days, the way your physical body is formed — is praise for God the first thing that comes to mind? Not only did God form each molecule in your body, he laid out all aspects of your life before you were even born — your family, your future career, your fear, and your failures. It is easy to look in the mirror and to be discontent — with the flaws in your facial features or the discontentment in your daily tasks. What should change when you reflect on the fact that there is no aspect of your life unknown to God?

PRAY

Don't just praise God for abstract concepts today. Praise him for the specific ways he has shown his power in your life and ordained your steps. Praise him for the parts of your life that are obviously good, the parts of your personality that you struggle with or fear, and even the past that formed you. God ordained it all! Thank him for forming each detail of your story, and ask for continued courage. Trust that you are a *good* work made by God, no matter what circumstances surround you.

LIVE

God has prepared the day you are about to live. God crafted you, inside and out, to live it. Go.

DON'T PUSH

PHILIPPIANS 2:1-4

1-4   If you've gotten anything at all out of following Christ, if his love has made any difference in your life, if being in a community of the Spirit means anything to you, if you have a heart, if you *care*—then do me a favor: Agree with each other, love each other, be deep-spirited friends. Don't push your way to the front; don't sweet-talk your way to the top. Put yourself aside, and help others get ahead. Don't be obsessed with getting your own advantage. Forget yourselves long enough to lend a helping hand.

READ

Read the passage slowly, letting the words sink in.

THINK

You might not think of yourself as ambitious. Few are outwardly or openly vying for power, especially women in a church setting. However, survival instincts are stronger than you think. Insecurity might make you do and say little things to put yourself ever-so-slightly forward. It might be a mention of what the other person didn't do or an extra emphasis on what you did. These are the very things that disrupt deep-spirited friendships. How are you tempted to put yourself ahead or seek your own advantage? What is the deeper cause of those motivations?

PRAY

Confess to God the places where you've fallen short and sought your own advantage at others' expense. Ask him how to make amends so your life is full of agreement with others instead of competition. Ask for the grace you and others need to "forget yourselves long enough to lend a helping hand." Intercede for those you have hurt or for those who have hurt you. Ask for the transforming love of Christ.

LIVE

Putting others before yourself isn't an abstract process. It happens with the choices that you make. Consciously choose to put your own advantage last today with someone that you encounter. Instead focus on loving them well.

GLORY-STRENGTH

COLOSSIANS 1:9-14

9-12   Be assured that from the first day we heard of you, we haven't stopped praying for you, asking God to give you wise minds and spirits attuned to his will, and so acquire a thorough understanding of the ways in which God works. We pray that you'll live well for the Master, making him proud of you as you work hard in his orchard. As you learn more and more how God works, you will learn how to do *your* work. We pray that you'll have the strength to stick it out over the long haul — not the grim strength of gritting your teeth but the glory-strength God gives. It is strength that endures the unendurable and spills over into joy, thanking the Father who makes us strong enough to take part in everything bright and beautiful that he has for us.

13-14   God rescued us from dead-end alleys and dark dungeons. He's set us up in the kingdom of the Son he loves so much, the Son who got us out of the pit we were in, got rid of the sins we were doomed to keep repeating.

READ

Read the passage slowly aloud to yourself. Try to truly imagine the word pictures presented.

THINK

Consider how your work relates to God's work. Paul includes a sampling of God's work in the last verses — search and rescue, intervention, and redemption. If God, the good gardener, is working toward these things, how does he invite you to be a part of that? Why does Paul ask for strength, and what type of specific perseverance does he ask for? What is the difference between enduring a necessary task and doing something difficult with someone you love? What is all the hard work in this passage preparing us for?

PRAY

Picture God's orchard and your place in it. Praise the Lord for the chance to be a part of his good work. Confess where you feel in need of strength — weariness is a normal part of being human. Ask for his strength as you go about producing fruit, whether that be in your vocation, your relationships, or your spiritual walk with him.

LIVE

Write down some times when you feel certain God has given you his "glory-strength" and brought you into joy. What fruit did he produce?

_____

_____

_____

RESPECT FOR CHRIST IN ACTION

EPHESIANS 5:21-28

21 Out of respect for Christ, be courteously reverent to one another.

22-24 Wives, understand and support your husbands in ways that show your support for Christ. The husband provides leadership to his wife the way Christ does to his church, not by domineering but by cherishing. So just as the church submits to Christ as he exercises such leadership, wives should likewise submit to their husbands.

25-28 Husbands, go all out in your love for your wives, exactly as Christ did for the church — a love marked by giving, not getting. Christ's love makes the church whole. His words evoke her beauty. Everything he does and says is designed to bring the best out of her, dressing her in dazzling white silk, radiant with holiness. And that is how husbands ought to love their wives. They're really doing themselves a favor — since they're already "one" in marriage.

READ

Read this passage slowly and carefully, attentive to the details and the tone of the author's language. Try not to jump to conclusions based on pre-conceptions. Observe. Receive. Reflect.

THINK

The umbrella command that encompasses both husbands and wives in this passage is to be "courteously reverent" to one another. The word "reverence" is much more than simply kindness or compatibility. Usually it's a word used of a divine figure. In this case, it describes a deep understanding and awareness of the eternal value of the soul of your spouse. From that perspective, what do you think Paul means to suggest about the wife in a marriage relationship? How is that reflected in, and in some ways dependent on, the behavior of the husband?

PRAY

Write your own prayer of confession, thanks, and supplication related to your relationship. Consider how you can support in a way that shows your support for Christ.

_____

_____

_____

LIVE

As human beings, and especially as women, manipulation is incredibly tempting. Control is easier than loving service, and control gives the illusion of security. However, security that is bought by nagging or twisting is just that — the illusion of safety, which actually covers a deeper ache and emptiness. Live and love with great freedom, with "a love marked by giving, not getting."

15

MISSING GOD

JOHN 8:21-26

21 Then he went over the same ground again. "I'm leaving and you are going to look for me, but you're missing God in this and are headed for a dead end. There is no way you can come with me."

22 The Jews said, "So, is he going to kill himself? Is that what he means by 'You can't come with me'?"

23-24 Jesus said, "You're tied down to the mundane; I'm in touch with what is beyond your horizons. You live in terms of what you see and touch. I'm living on other terms. I told you that you were missing God in all this. You're at a dead end. If you won't believe I am who I say I am, you're at the dead end of sins. You're missing God in your lives."

25-26 They said to him, "Just who are you anyway?"

Jesus said, "What I've said from the start. I have so many things to say that concern you, judgments to make that affect you, but if you don't accept the trustworthiness of the One who commanded my words and acts, none of it matters. That is who you are questioning—not me but the One who sent me."

READ

Try to understand the questions of the crowd at Christ's puzzling words. Read the passage slowly through, pausing before each portion of dialogue.

THINK

Although Christ's words were directed to the disbelieving Jews in front of him, they are still sacred words that pierce our hearts today. Jesus says that unless you believe who he claims to be, you are at a dead end spiritually. Although you might have known Jesus for years, do you still find yourself sometimes asking who he really is in your life? Do you too wonder if you might be "missing God in all this"? What does Jesus claim to be — not just in the lives of the ancient Jews, but in your life today? Have you stopped struggling to believe beyond "what you see and touch" and trusted the One who "is beyond your horizons"?

PRAY

Ask God to reveal the dead ends in your life. Examine the disbelief that got you there. Confess the parts of Christ's lordship that you find easy to talk about and hard to truly live. Praise God for his revelation in Jesus — speak aloud as many of his attributes as you can think of. Ask for the ability to "accept the trustworthiness" of God.

LIVE

Jesus' claim to be Savior and Risen One does not just change our spiritual Sunday beliefs — it changes everything and turns dead ends into bridges. What aspect of your life today will you change knowing that Jesus is who he says he is?

THE WAY GOD WORKS

ISAIAH 55:8-11

8-11   "I don't think the way you think.
      The way you work isn't the way I work."
         GOD's Decree.
"For as the sky soars high above earth,
     so the way I work surpasses the way you work,
     and the way I think is beyond the way you think.
Just as rain and snow descend from the skies
     and don't go back until they've watered the earth,
Doing their work of making things grow and blossom,
     producing seed for farmers and food for the hungry,
So will the words that come out of my mouth
     not come back empty-handed.
They'll do the work I sent them to do,
     they'll complete the assignment I gave them."

READ

Read the passage aloud slowly. Pause to picture each metaphor.

THINK

The background of this passage includes God's work of painful redemption — Israel has been exiled to Babylon for her sins and will not be freed for some time. The fact that God's work is very different from our own does not just mean a different time line or desired outcome. Sometimes it means a method that you could never have foreseen, a process of growth that you would reject as too painful, too cruel, or too ineffective. Why do you think God uses the seasons, the weather, and the growth of nature to portray his works and his words?

PRAY

Confess the ways that you have been frustrated with God's work in the past. How have your prioritized your ways over God's? Be honest about your failure to trust God's ultimately good purposes. Praise God for the way his mind is beyond and above your own. Thank him for working for better things than you can understand. Surrender your narrow view of how things "should be done" in your life today.

LIVE

What is your "work" today? Given God's work in your life, what will you change about your own way of accomplishing that work? How will trust change your steps?

DON'T FORGET

DEUTERONOMY 4:7-9,11-13

7-8   Yes. What other great nation has gods that are intimate with them the way GOD, our God, is with us, always ready to listen to us? And what other great nation has rules and regulations as good and fair as this Revelation that I'm setting before you today?

9   Just make sure you stay alert. Keep close watch over yourselves. Don't forget anything of what you've seen. Don't let your heart wander off. Stay vigilant as long as you live. Teach what you've seen and heard to your children and grandchildren. . . .

11-13   You gathered. You stood in the shadow of the mountain. The mountain was ablaze with fire, blazing high into the very heart of Heaven. You stood in deep darkness and thick clouds. GOD spoke to you out of the fire. You heard the sound of words but you saw nothing — no form, only a voice. He announced his covenant, the Ten Words, by which he commanded you to live. Then he wrote them down on two slabs of stone.

READ

Read the passage aloud slowly. Try to visualize the experiences described, whether past or future.

THINK

As Moses prepares the Israelites to cross the Jordan, he does not begin a list of new expectations for the new land. Instead he commands in a variety of ways that the Israelites remember the past and all that God has done for them, both as a nation and personally. Compared to other ideas about "divinity" as a distant orderer of the universe, God is intimately involved in the lives of his people. Although it would seem pretty hard to forget parting oceans and pillars of fire, God emphasizes the importance of memory through Moses. It is tempting to think "big" miracles would be easier landmarks, but has God already moved in your life in big ways? Moses doesn't just remind the Israelites of abstract qualities of God — he reminds them of where they were, and how God interacted with them.

PRAY

Bring your heart and mind back to the places where God clearly intervened in your life, no matter how large or small. As you focus on that memory, praise God for the specific ways he revealed himself to you. Reflect on his role in your redemption and well-being. Respond in thanksgiving again and ask God to continue to reveal himself in clear ways that you can remember. Ask for the courage and excitement to tell this tale to others.

LIVE

What would your legacy of God's work sound like as a story? How will you remember God's movement in your life as a mighty act and not simply a distant idea?

18

FLOURISHING LOVE

PHILIPPIANS 1:9-11

9-11 So this is my prayer: that your love will flourish and that you will not only love much but well. Learn to love appropriately. You need to use your head and test your feelings so that your love is sincere and intelligent, not sentimental gush. Live a lover's life, circumspect and exemplary, a life Jesus will be proud of: bountiful in fruits from the soul, making Jesus Christ attractive to all, getting everyone involved in the glory and praise of God.

READ

Imagine reading this to someone very dear to you. Read it with tenderness, wishing every ounce of blessing possible upon them.

THINK

Generally the epistles address or correct certain "problems" in the community of believers. What sort of things might Paul be trying to correct in his audience and therefore in us? Paul discusses not just quantity of love, but quality, using words like "sincere," "bountiful," "attractive," and "intelligent" to describe it. What do you think it takes for true Christian love like this to really flourish?

PRAY

Examine carefully the "love" you proclaim toward those in your Christian community and those outside of it. Does it meet the description Paul gives? Confess the ways you see your love falling short. Remember that it is only Christ's divine love and grace that allow us to love the way we should. Ask for a sense of limitless, abundant, gospel love to flood over into the way you love others. Don't be anxious about making Christ look attractive — his love makes everyone beautiful and even covers our mistakes.

LIVE

Who are you going to love "sincerely" today? What obstacles stand in the way of that endeavor, and how will you look to Christ to overcome them?

KINGDOM EQUALITY

JAMES 2:1-6

1-4 My dear friends, don't let public opinion influence how you live out our glorious, Christ-originated faith. If a man enters your church wearing an expensive suit, and a street person wearing rags comes in right after him, and you say to the man in the suit, "Sit here, sir; this is the best seat in the house!" and either ignore the street person or say, "Better sit here in the back row," haven't you segregated God's children and proved that you are judges who can't be trusted?

5-6 Listen, dear friends. Isn't it clear by now that God operates quite differently? He chose the world's down-and-out as the kingdom's first citizens, with full rights and privileges. The kingdom is promised to anyone who loves God. And here you are abusing these same citizens!

♪ Give me your eyes ♪ - Brandon Heath

Give me your love for humanity.

READ

Imagine the different voices as you read—separate between the voice of the writer and the voices of the folks in church he is imitating. What emotions are prevalent?

THINK

It is hard to imagine something as obviously snobbish as snubbing the poorly dressed. Think carefully, however, about the ways that status and society invade our church behavior. Isn't it easier to have coffee with the person your age instead of that strange older person? Although we may not avoid those low on cash, don't we often skirt around those poor in social skills? Is that avoidance very much different? Think carefully about James' statement about the kingdom of God. How does God's system contrast the way the world views people?

PRAY

Ask God for the vision of Jesus Christ and not society's standards when you look at the "least of these." Confess where you have been guided by the subtle pressures of status and popularity. Pray for the generosity of spirit that furthers the kingdom, and pray over specific people in your community that you struggle to love.

LIVE

Jesus always brings in those on the fringes of society as the foremost citizens of his kingdom, because they understand a need for grace and unconditional love that "together" people cannot. Identify yourself with them. Today, don't just give lip service to love.

COMPARING AND COMPETING

1 CORINTHIANS 4:7-8

7-8   For who do you know that really knows *you*, knows your heart? And even if they did, is there anything they would discover in you that you could take credit for? Isn't everything you *have* and everything you *are* sheer gifts from God? So what's the point of all this comparing and competing? You already have all you need. You already have more access to God than you can handle. Without bringing either Apollos or me into it, you're sitting on top of the world — at least God's world — and we're right there, sitting alongside you!

READ

Pause after each question in the text. Honestly pose the questions to yourself — don't just rush through as though these were statements.

THINK

With whom and when do you feel the need to compare and compete? Be honest — none of us are exempt in this very achievement-based society. If even your best accomplishment is simply a gift from God, then even your greatest weakness is not enough to take you down. How does this change how you perceive others, especially those more "spiritual" than you?

PRAY

Come humbly before God. Confess the need you feel to explain or justify yourself to others — explore the unintentional ways you might twist words or situations to make yourself look "in the right." Ask God to help you break that bad habit. Entreat him for true confidence in your identity as his child.

LIVE

Think about the place or group of people with whom you feel the most insecure. Act in trust today, rather than in fear. Don't compete — walk forward in gratitude for all the good things you *have* been given.

NOW AND NOT YET

1 PETER 1:2-5

2   God the Father has his eye on each of you, and has determined by the work of the Spirit to keep you obedient through the sacrifice of Jesus. May everything good from God be yours!

3-5   What a God we have! And how fortunate we are to have him, this Father of our Master Jesus! Because Jesus was raised from the dead, we've been given a brand-new life and have everything to live for, including a future in heaven — and the future starts now! God is keeping careful watch over us and the future. The Day is coming when you'll have it all — life healed and whole.

READ

Read the passage aloud with expression. Linger on the words "fortunate," "future," "life," "healed," and "whole."

THINK

There are two ideas that seem to be in tension with one another here: "the Day is coming" and "the future starts now." If Jesus' death and resurrection have secured the future, what tastes of heaven do we see here and now? If "the Day" is still coming, what is it that we are still missing? Where do you still feel longing in your own life?

PRAY

Ask God to reveal your fortune in Christ. Praise him for a new life made possible "through the sacrifice of Jesus," and specifically the ways you see the newness and glory marching into your everyday reality. Confess what you are still longing for, and ask earnestly for all that you still hope.

LIVE

Now that you have been reminded of the reality of the future touching your everyday life, how will you walk today like heaven is moments from you? No matter what comes your way today, keep reminding yourself that "everything good from God" is yours for the savoring right now.

RELATIONSHIPS WITH THE WOUNDED

RUTH 1:11-17

11-13 But Naomi was firm: "Go back, my dear daughters. Why would you come with me? Do you suppose I still have sons in my womb who can become your future husbands? Go back, dear daughters — on your way, please! I'm too old to get a husband. Why, even if I said, 'There's still hope!' and this very night got a man and had sons, can you imagine being satisfied to wait until they were grown? Would you wait that long to get married again? No, dear daughters; this is a bitter pill for me to swallow — more bitter for me than for you. GOD has dealt me a hard blow."

14 Again they cried openly. Orpah kissed her mother-in-law good-bye; but Ruth embraced her and held on.

15 Naomi said, "Look, your sister-in-law is going back home to live with her own people and gods; go with her."

16-17 But Ruth said, "Don't force me to leave you; don't make me go home. Where you go, I go; and where you live, I'll live. Your people are my people, your God is my god; where you die, I'll die, and that's where I'll be buried, so help me GOD — not even death itself is going to come between us!"

READ

Read the story with emotion, expected and unexpected.

THINK

Imagine the scene: Naomi is in a foreign land and she has lost all of her closest kin. She is insisting Ruth leave, but why? Consider what you know about those in the process of suffering deep pain. Now think carefully about what was at stake for Ruth. While Naomi was returning to her native land, Ruth was leaving "home" to follow her. In that time, marriage was not just about companionship — it was akin to the basic, simple security of being employed. Naomi reminds Ruth she has nothing to offer — no financial security, no certainty, and not even emotional comfort. In fact, Naomi feels her heart and life are brimming with only bad, bitter things. What kind of a gift could that be? When Ruth refuses to leave, she refuses to be detached from Naomi's pain. She proclaims the gift of relationship is stronger than the uncertainty it might bring. She "held on." Who do you most identify with in this passage?

PRAY

Consider the wounds and losses you have received and the grief of those in your community. Ask God for guidance and grace to receive comfort and companionship as well as to offer it where and when it is needed. Thank him for the gift of deep community, especially among women.

LIVE

Write out the names of Ruths and Naomis in your life. How will you follow them into their difficulties and allow them to follow you into yours?

_____

_____

_____

LIVE CREATIVELY

GALATIANS 6:1-5

1-3 Live creatively, friends. If someone falls into sin, forgivingly restore him, saving your critical comments for yourself. *You* might be needing forgiveness before the day's out. Stoop down and reach out to those who are oppressed. Share their burdens, and so complete Christ's law. If you think you are too good for that, you are badly deceived.

4-5 Make a careful exploration of who you are and the work you have been given, and then sink yourself into that. Don't be impressed with yourself. Don't compare yourself with others. Each of you must take responsibility for doing the creative best you can with your own life.

READ

Read the passage aloud. What phrases stand out to you? What vivid verbs show the course of action?

THINK

Paul tells his readers to think carefully about "who you are and the work you have been given." Having a firm sense of identity is essential to living creatively and lovingly. If you are overly anxious about your accomplishments or overly critical of others' failures, you do not have an understanding of Christ's love and power. You are a unique individual, called by God to certain tasks, given certain strengths and certain weaknesses — but not for your own success. Your individual ministry is "given" to you, not assigned in punishment. So, what is the purpose of *your* life and calling? Are you working to stoop down and lift others' burdens? Are you taking responsibility for a life brimming with forgiveness and restoration?

PRAY

Repent of your comparisons. Whether it's with other people or even some ideal of yourself, whatever is not "the work you have been given" has got to go. Ask God to forgive the lack of trust. Request a heart to restore and lift up those who are burdened.

LIVE

What is the work you have been given today? How will you "live creatively," considering the burdens of others as you do so?

WATCH YOUR WORDS

EPHESIANS 4:29-32

29 Watch the way you talk. Let nothing foul or dirty come out of your mouth. Say only what helps, each word a gift.

30 Don't grieve God. Don't break his heart. His Holy Spirit, moving and breathing in you, is the most intimate part of your life, making you fit for himself. Don't take such a gift for granted.

31-32 Make a clean break with all cutting, backbiting, profane talk. Be gentle with one another, sensitive. Forgive one another as quickly and thoroughly as God in Christ forgave you.

READ

Read the passage through once slowly and silently. Then read it aloud to yourself, pausing after each phrase.

THINK

This passage quite simply is a list of dos and don'ts. However, the warnings have to do with God's work in your life, while the positive commandments are specifically about speech. How are those two concepts connected? Do you think of your words as simply a way to express what you need to? How much thought goes into your speech before it comes out of your mouth? Although it might be tempting to see speaking as just "something we do," it is clear that to God words are valuable — a way to communicate grace or judgment, love or pain. In fact, sometimes falsely "kind" words are far worse than the honest rebuke from someone who loves you. What does it mean to be gentle and yet honest? How will you use your words to help, but also not to enable sinful behavior?

PRAY

Repent of your words that have not helped, and forgive those who have wounded you with their own insensitive phrases. Beg God for mercy to use words wisely in a culture that doesn't value clear communication. Ask God for the help of the Spirit in making every word a gift.

LIVE

Write the names of a few key people you will speak with today. How will you make your words to them not only gentle and sensitive but meaning-ful? Craft a "word gift" to share with each of them.

_____

_____

_____

GOD IS GREATER THAN YOUR WORRIED HEART

1 JOHN 3:18-22

18-20 My dear children, let's not just talk about love; let's practice real love. This is the only way we'll know we're living truly, living in God's reality. It's also the way to shut down debilitating self-criticism, even when there is something to it. For God is greater than our worried hearts and knows more about us than we do ourselves.

21-22 And friends, once that's taken care of and we're no longer accusing or condemning ourselves, we're bold and free before God! We're able to stretch our hands out and receive what we asked for because we're doing what he said, doing what pleases him.

READ

Read the passage through once silently to get a sense of the tone. Then, read it again aloud. Preach it to yourself.

THINK

Do you know anything about "debilitating self-criticism"? If you're stuck beating yourself up for your failures and your shortcomings, "even when there is something to it," you're missing a key point of the gospel. God knows you — every detail, every flaw and weakness — even better than you could know yourself. And yet, his love is greater than your worried heart and your insufficient actions. To hang on to those mistakes betrays a lack of trust in the absolute power of God's grace. Not only that, it keeps you from loving others — it keeps you from receiving all that God wants to give and going where God wants to send you.

PRAY

Confess to God the self-criticism that you are stuck in. Whether it is broad or one very specific shackle, ask him to free you from obsessing with it. Surrender it to Christ and ask for that space to be filled with love in practice for God and for others.

LIVE

Write out some of your top, nagging self-criticisms and how they specifically have kept you from effectively entering into God's plan of love. After writing them out, keep a watch for them creeping into your interactions today.

_____

_____

_____

CAREFUL AND CAREFREE

1 PETER 5:4-7

4-5   When God, who is the best shepherd of all, comes out in the open with his rule, he'll see that you've done it right and commend you lavishly. And you who are younger must follow your leaders. But all of you, leaders and followers alike, are to be down to earth with each other, for —

> God has had it with the proud,
> But takes delight in just plain people.

6-7   So be content with who you are, and don't put on airs. God's strong hand is on you; he'll promote you at the right time. Live carefree before God; he is most careful with you.

READ

Read the passage aloud slowly. After some time for silent reflection, read it again to yourself. What words and phrases stand out?

THINK

Do you remember the last time you felt content with who you are? With the wonderful responsibilities and changes of adulthood comes a certain loss of innocence. You might have started to see your body, your family situation, your social skills, and your talents only in comparison with others — others who had less, more, or something you did not have at all. How much of your time and energy goes into trying to change who you are, especially as a woman? Compensating for your weaknesses, trying extra hard to play up your strengths? If God has shaped your life, knowing you before time began, maybe you can really trust him with who you are — after all, he is the "most careful with you." What do you think that word "careful" might mean here, based on the character of God?

PRAY

Ask God to reveal who you truly are — who he made you to be. Confess your insecurities, the places where it seems his hand isn't strong enough to overcome your flaws. Implore the Lord for the strength to "live carefree" in the knowledge of his power.

LIVE

In whose company are you most tempted to "put on airs"? Remind yourself of "God's strong hand" on you today when you encounter them. Be yourself, "live carefree."

GOD IS READY TO HELP

HEBREWS 13:5-8

5-6   Don't be obsessed with getting more material things. Be relaxed with what you have. Since God assured us, "I'll never let you down, never walk off and leave you," we can boldly quote,

> God is there, ready to help;
> I'm fearless no matter what.
> Who or what can get to me?

7-8   Appreciate your pastoral leaders who gave you the Word of God. Take a good look at the way they live, and let their faithfulness instruct you, as well as their truthfulness. There should be a consistency that runs through us all. For Jesus doesn't change — yesterday, today, tomorrow, he's always totally himself.

READ

Read the words aloud with tender affection.

THINK

How many trusted people have let you down? How many have been unsupportive or simply not present at all? You might have learned to always keep your guard up for sheer survival. In this constantly changing, incredibly fast culture, it is easy to live expecting financial, relational, and emotional blows. But Jesus promises what no other human being can: that he will never leave you and that he will never change. His love is constant, and his support is unfailing. The abandonment that you fear so deeply is the opposite of his character. Not only is Christ not going to walk away, he will always be walking after you. Even if you try to leave, he will find you — yesterday, today, tomorrow — whether you're in church and in good spirits or in a corner of broken doubt on your knees.

PRAY

Praise and thank Christ for his unchanging and constant love. Confess the abandonment you fear most. What are you afraid will change and leave you alone? Ask for help forgiving those who have left you feeling unable to trust. Ask God to speak into that fear with a sense of his absolute trustworthiness.

LIVE

Although the world is changing quickly, Paul suggests we should strive to imitate some of Christ's consistency. From a sense of God's unchanging love, how will you practice constancy today in your life and in your love of others?

BOTH FEET PLANTED

EPHESIANS 3:10,14-21

10   Through followers of Jesus like yourselves gathered in churches, this extraordinary plan of God is becoming known and talked about even among the angels! . . .

14-19   My response is to get down on my knees before the Father, this magnificent Father who parcels out all heaven and earth. I ask him to strengthen you by his Spirit—not a brute strength but a glorious inner strength—that Christ will live in you as you open the door and invite him in. And I ask him that with both feet planted firmly on love, you'll be able to take in with all followers of Jesus the extravagant dimensions of Christ's love. Reach out and experience the breadth! Test its length! Plumb the depths! Rise to the heights! Live full lives, full in the fullness of God.

20-21   God can do anything, you know—far more than you could ever imagine or guess or request in your wildest dreams! He does it not by pushing us around but by working within us, his Spirit deeply and gently within us.

READ

This passage is a prayer. Try not to be distracted by punctuation as you read aloud. Instead let it flow as one continuous thought. If you would like, read the passage again, replacing "you" with the name of someone on your heart.

THINK

Each member of the Trinity is mentioned in this passage. What role does each seem to have? How does the power of God the Creator relate to the strength of the Spirit and the love of Christ? Notice that Paul's prayer for those he loves is all bound up with descriptions of God's character — who he is and what he does. What exactly is it that Paul is asking for — what are the parts of this prayer? What seem to be the requests of God and what seem to be the encouraged actions of the believers? Pick one phrase in this prayer and delve deeply into the possibilities.

PRAY

Like Paul, ask God for a revelation of the unbelievable, limitless love of Jesus Christ. Ask for strength, for the freedom to live "fully" and not just out of a sense of duty. Praise God for his incredible ability to do anything and so much more than we can imagine, and then ask him for all you can hope for, knowing that you can trust in his boundless love and care for you.

LIVE

Formulate your own prayer that addresses God the Father, Son, and Holy Spirit. What kind of life and love do you want to ask for?

_____

_____

_____

BURSTING WITH GOD-NEWS

LUKE 1:46-55

46-55   Mary said,

I'm bursting with God-news;
    I'm dancing the song of my Savior God.
God took one good look at me, and look what happened —
    I'm the most fortunate woman on earth!
What God has done for me will never be forgotten,
    the God whose very name is holy, set apart from all others.
His mercy flows in wave after wave
    on those who are in awe before him.
He bared his arm and showed his strength,
    scattered the bluffing braggarts.
He knocked tyrants off their high horses,
    pulled victims out of the mud.
The starving poor sat down to a banquet;
    the callous rich were left out in the cold.
He embraced his chosen child, Israel;
    he remembered and piled on the mercies, piled them high.
It's exactly what he promised,
    beginning with Abraham and right up to now.

READ

These verses follow Mary's visit from the angel, when she was told she would miraculously bear Jesus despite her virginity. This is her song when Elizabeth, her cousin, greets and praises her character and God's. Read it with expression the way you would sing an enthusiastic song of praise.

THINK

Just before this outburst, Mary's cousin praises her because she "believed what God said, believed every word would come true!" Would you respond to Mary's calling with as much joy as she did? Here was a very young girl called to play a *very* important role — but with the risk of losing her community's (and her boyfriend's!) respect and support. With the announcement Mary is to bear a son who will rule Israel forever, her song reflects the "politics" of God's kingdom. What does Mary's song reveal about her understanding of God?

PRAY

Take Mary's song of joy and thanks and make it into a personal prayer, replacing "God" with "you." Mary was reflecting on a specific intervention of God in her life. Add to your prayer of thanks specific memories of how God has moved in your world and piled mercy upon mercy.

LIVE

How will you reflect God's politics today? His Spirit is in you — all of the actions Mary described are happening in your life as well.

TAKE A BREAK

MARK 6:30-32

30-31   The apostles then rendezvoused with Jesus and reported on all that they had done and taught. Jesus said, "Come off by yourselves; let's take a break and get a little rest." For there was constant coming and going. They didn't even have time to eat.

32   So they got in the boat and went off to a remote place by themselves.

READ

This passage comes after the disciples venture off on their own to heal in the Spirit and before the feeding of the five thousand. Read with that context in mind. Read slowly, trying to observe all of the relational detail.

THINK

Jesus is not in the business of overworking you. Sure, he has not called you to a life of leisure. But God is also aware of your humanity. He wants you to go when he sends you, to rest when he commands, and most importantly to seek balance because of your trust in him rather than your own frantic efforts. Participating in the work of the kingdom is an invitation to be present with Jesus — not an excuse to abuse your body and spirit with constant rush. Stop. Listen. Think. Would you be willing to rest and break away from your important work if Jesus asked you to?

PRAY

Lay out all of your to-do lists before God today. Take a moment and rest in his presence. Remember that he is looking out for your needs — physical, emotional, and spiritual — even when you forget about them. Praise him for his care, and ask for wisdom to discern between hard work and needless hustle and stress.

LIVE

You have been reminded that God cares about your health and your needs — that you are supposed to find a balance between work and rest, draining and recharging. You are not the only one struggling, forgetting to eat and take time alone. Encourage someone in your path who seems overworked that rest matters — offer a space for them to receive that stillness.

HIS UNFOLDING GRACE

2 CORINTHIANS 4:16-18

16-18   So we're not giving up. How could we! Even though on the outside it often looks like things are falling apart on us, on the inside, where God is making new life, not a day goes by without his unfolding grace. These hard times are small potatoes compared to the coming good times, the lavish celebration prepared for us. There's far more here than meets the eye. The things we see now are here today, gone tomorrow. But the things we can't see now will last forever.

READ

Try to strike the balance between cheerleader (too much sugar) and football coach (too much gruffness) here. Read this aloud to yourself in a tone of encouragement.

THINK

When life around us seems to be falling apart, it can be harder and harder to believe the truth about your identity in Christ and his coming kingdom. Note that Paul doesn't just talk about the hard times *eventually* ending. Instead, he reminds us that the hard times are going to be replaced with something unimaginably better than a lack of pain: a celebration, "unfolding grace," and "new life." Even though some of those things are yet to come, the seeds of those good things have already been planted in your life. They are growing every day, no matter what surrounds you.

PRAY

Do you feel like giving up? Like things are falling apart or beyond redemption? Cry out to God for a change in perspective, so that you can see that your "hard times are small potatoes compared to the coming good times." Ask him to show you evidence of the new life he is making within you.

LIVE

"Not a day goes by without his unfolding grace." As you enter your routine today refuse to see the difficulties you encounter as anything but grace.

FROM START TO FINISH

EPHESIANS 2:7-10

7-10   Now God has us where he wants us, with all the time in this world and the next to shower grace and kindness upon us in Christ Jesus. Saving is all his idea, and all his work. All we do is trust him enough to let him do it. It's God's gift from start to finish! We don't play the major role. If we did, we'd probably go around bragging that we'd done the whole thing! No, we neither make nor save ourselves. God does both the making and saving. He creates each of us by Christ Jesus to join him in the work he does, the good work he has gotten ready for us to do, work we had better be doing.

READ

Read the passage slowly once through. Pause for silent reflection as you let this unfamiliar version of this familiar text sink in. Then read it again.

THINK

If someone asks you where or when you were saved, you might describe a moment — at summer camp or in church — when you accepted grace. How does this passage portray the true nature and origin of salvation? God certainly does offer an invitation, and while you might be able to remember saying yes, it is ultimately his party from start to finish — crafted in your life long before you could *do* anything. Our part was simple: receiving and thanksgiving. However, although our sins are gone, the work isn't done yet — "the good work he has gotten ready for us to do" is the "work we had better be doing."

PRAY

Praise God for his glorious idea of salvation. You could never have thought of the where, the how, the when, or the people who brought it about. Thank God for his care and foresight, which show all the detail of a surprise from someone you love, times infinity. Give Jesus all of the credit. Ask God for guidance, joy, and courage as you walk beyond a "salvation moment" and into the future "salvation work" prepared for you.

LIVE

Consider "the good work" that God has prepared for you, whether it is simply a daily encounter or a lifelong mission field. Walk confidently forward, knowing that God has the "big stuff" covered and planned out.

PRAY VERY SIMPLY

MATTHEW 6:7-13

7-13   The world is full of so-called prayer warriors who are prayer-ignorant. They're full of formulas and programs and advice, peddling techniques for getting what you want from God. Don't fall for that nonsense. This is your Father you are dealing with, and he knows better than you what you need. With a God like this loving you, you can pray very simply. Like this:

> Our Father in heaven,
> Reveal who you are.
> Set the world right;
> Do what's best —
>   as above, so below.
> Keep us alive with three square meals.
> Keep us forgiven with you and forgiving others.
> Keep us safe from ourselves and the Devil.
> You're in charge!
> You can do anything you want!
> You're ablaze in beauty!
>   Yes. Yes. Yes.

READ

Read the passage aloud with the expression you imagine Jesus might have used.

THINK

Christ asks us to come simply, directly, and honestly before God — asking for what we need, not beating around the bush and not forgetting praise alongside requests. To the disciples Jesus spoke to, addressing God as "Father" and asking him for "three square meals" might have seemed irreverent. What does it truly mean that God is your Father, however? How does that affect the way you speak to him? What do you think Jesus means when he talks about "prayer warriors" with formulas?

PRAY

Pray, first using these words provided by Jesus and then adding your own. Keep it short, simple, and direct. Skip the "Christianese" that creeps in. It's just you and God.

LIVE

Journal out some of the simplest and sweetest prayer phrases in your own words that truly express your heart's desire. Look back on these when your words seem to dry up.

_____

_____

_____

WHAT A GOD!

PSALM 18:28-34

28-29   Suddenly, GOD, you floodlight my life;
     I'm blazing with glory, God's glory!
I smash the bands of marauders,
     I vault the highest fences.

30   What a God! His road
     stretches straight and smooth.
Every GOD-direction is road-tested.
     Everyone who runs toward him
Makes it.

31-34   Is there any god like GOD?
     Are we not at bedrock?
Is not this the God who armed me,
     then aimed me in the right direction?
Now I run like a deer;
     I'm king of the mountain.
He shows me how to fight;
     I can bend a bronze bow!

READ

This passage is meant to be sung, presumably with jubilation and upbeat tempo. In lieu of music, read it aloud with expression.

THINK

The salvation of God is not simply a rescue. It is a powerful, strength-giving experience. The psalmist sings of smashing, vaulting, running, fighting, and bending bows of bronze! It's hard not to think of superheroes. Do you associate salvation with pure, unadulterated strength and power? Or are you inclined to think salvation merely makes us nicer or less sinful? Do not misunderstand — there is a power in absolute Christlike kindness, but it is not passive and it is certainly not just a thought or a theory. The salvation of God is arming you for battle, showing you how to fight. What fight is God preparing you for?

PRAY

Thank God for his divine salvation, which is a truly miraculous, empowering, and strengthening force in your life. Not only has God rescued you, he has prepared you for great things. Ask him to "aim" you in the right direction and to show you what his strength is meant for in your life. Ask him to give the strength of salvation to others who are feeling battle-weary and in need of illumination. Fight the battle against evil with good courage.

LIVE

Whether your energy today is low or high, whether the tasks ahead are simple or seemingly impossible, remember that God's salvation is a source of strength bigger and deeper and stronger than your circumstances.

A PRAISEWORTHY WOMAN

PROVERBS 31:25-30

25-30   When she speaks she has something worthwhile to say,
and she always says it kindly.
She keeps an eye on everyone in her household,
and keeps them all busy and productive.
Her children respect and bless her;
her husband joins in with words of praise:
"Many women have done wonderful things,
but you've outclassed them all!"
Charm can mislead and beauty soon fades.
The woman to be admired and praised
is the woman who lives in the Fear-of-God.

READ

Read this familiar passage slowly and carefully. Abandon your preconceptions from sermons and books. Imagine you are friends with this woman; what might she be like and how would these descriptions play out in reality?

THINK

If this passage is a list of things to do, it is completely overwhelming and arguably impossible. Running a household and simply living an adult woman's life in our culture is more hectic and weighed down with "shoulds" than ever before — and this proverb does not even include exercise! The key to understanding this passage, however, is in the last words — this is about a woman whose strength and character are not made up of the things that she is doing, but instead the personal God that she trusts in. None of the things she accomplishes would be possible without viewing her life as an act of service to a holy and powerful God who is always in control. All the rest is a natural outpouring.

PRAY

Ask God to help you understand in your heart what it means to pursue the fear of him in your daily life. Confess if you have been seeking charm, beauty, and productivity divorced from a worshipful attitude. Pray for the courage to not be overwhelmed by your tasks, but instead, seek to do them with a strength that comes from knowing who you are in relation to who God is. Ask for God to develop you into a woman who is worthy of praise, not for yourself, but to bring praise to the God who makes all of your efforts fruitful.

LIVE

Journal about how you want to become a woman who fears God today, specifically with the way you approach your daily tasks. Write reflectively about how knowing God reframes your to-do list.

_____

_____

_____

KEEP YOUR COOL

2 TIMOTHY 2:22-26

22-26 Run away from infantile indulgence. Run after mature righteousness — faith, love, peace — joining those who are in honest and serious prayer before God. Refuse to get involved in inane discussions; they always end up in fights. God's servant must not be argumentative, but a gentle listener and a teacher who keeps cool, working firmly but patiently with those who refuse to obey. You never know how or when God might sober them up with a change of heart and a turning to the truth, enabling them to escape the Devil's trap, where they are caught and held captive, forced to run his errands.

READ

Read the passage slowly aloud.

THINK

This passage is a balance of dos and don'ts. While it's important that we stop something bad, we must also run toward something good. Despite giving good directions on the type of company to seek, however, Paul does not tell his listeners to avoid the other sort of company. Instead, he gives good, concrete instruction on how to treat unproductive conversations and people — and more importantly, how to view "those who refuse to obey." What does Paul point out as unknown to us? What is the bigger spiritual picture in the lives of those we are tempted to have "inane discussions" with? How does that give you both confidence and compassion in dealing with bad conversations and bad company?

PRAY

Thank God for the spiritual battle that is already won. Draw into your mind those whose conversation does bring faith, love, and peace. Praise God for their presence in your life. Ask for strength, courage, and compassion to respond gently but firmly to those who try to tempt you, consciously or not, into fruitless discussions and arguments. Ask God to free them from the Devil's snares — the deeper, darker things that drive and motivate those negative words. Pray for guarded conversation and a loving, kind, but not enabling heart.

LIVE

Consider what scenarios in the day ahead are likely to produce fruitless arguments. How can you practice what Paul describes without being judgmental or unloving?

CREATIVITY AND ABUNDANCE

GENESIS 1:26-28

26-28 God spoke: "Let us make human beings in our image, make them
reflecting our nature
So they can be responsible for the fish in the sea,
the birds in the air, the cattle,
And, yes, Earth itself,
and every animal that moves on the face of Earth."
God created human beings;
he created them godlike,
Reflecting God's nature.
He created them male and female.
God blessed them:
"Prosper! Reproduce! Fill Earth! Take charge!
Be responsible for fish in the sea and birds in the air,
for every living thing that moves on the face of Earth."

READ

Read these familiar words slowly. Let them be new to you.

THINK

Although humanity has fallen away from this design, God's original intention for us still reveals his character and his beautiful desire. Notice the cause and effect in this passage, as God assigns responsibility with blessing. You are called to imitate his abundant and blessed creativity.

PRAY

Thank God for the beautiful burden of being made in his image. Ask God for direction in carrying out these commandments to cultivate and prosper in the "garden" that you are in.

LIVE

Write out a new conception of your responsibilities as a created and creative being made in God's image. You are part and parcel of God's own work in the world. How will you grow and prosper, not only for yourself, but to serve others?

_____

_____

_____

YOU'RE BLESSED

MATTHEW 5:1-5

1-2 When Jesus saw his ministry drawing huge crowds, he climbed a hillside. Those who were apprenticed to him, the committed, climbed with him. Arriving at a quiet place, he sat down and taught his climbing companions. This is what he said:

3 "You're blessed when you're at the end of your rope. With less of you there is more of God and his rule.

4 "You're blessed when you feel you've lost what is most dear to you. Only then can you be embraced by the One most dear to you.

5 "You're blessed when you're content with just who you are — no more, no less. That's the moment you find yourselves proud owners of everything that can't be bought."

READ

Read the passage carefully, allowing both the setting and the words to sink in. What do you think the original audience felt as they heard these words?

THINK

Most of our culture assumes that good things like wealth, health, and happiness come to good people. The world often defines "blessing" as success or simply a lack of turmoil. But Jesus has something more in mind. If blessings are a gift, what is required to "receive" the sort of blessing that Jesus describes? Note that these blessings apply no matter where you are in your life.

PRAY

Praise God for his character as a good giver and a gracious grower who only takes away so that he can increase what is most valuable. Confess to God any frustrations or fears you have, especially if you're at the end of your rope or experiencing loss. Ask him to make known to you the blessings he is working through those situations.

LIVE

Blessings come even in the form of losses, frustrations, and fears. Live today looking for God's mercies and goodness instead of focusing on what you think is missing.

DITCH THE EGO

GALATIANS 2:19-20

19-20 What actually took place is this: I tried keeping rules and working my head off to please God, and it didn't work. So I quit being a "law man" so that I could be *God's* man. Christ's life showed me how, and enabled me to do it. I identified myself completely with him. Indeed, I have been crucified with Christ. My ego is no longer central. It is no longer important that I appear righteous before you or have your good opinion, and I am no longer driven to impress God. Christ lives in me. The life you see me living is not "mine," but it is lived by faith in the Son of God, who loved me and gave himself for me. I am not going to go back on that.

READ

Read the passage slowly, allowing the words to sink in.

THINK

As a former Pharisee, Paul knows a thing or two about trying to keep rules to please God. While we may not have the same forms of obviously self-righteous behavior in our culture, there is still a very human tendency to try to create our own righteousness with good behavior. What are the "rules" that you try to keep to please God or make yourself look righteous in the company of others? What motivates such "rule-keeping" in your life? Why is it easier to have a checklist of good and bad behaviors than to identify completely with Christ?

PRAY

Confess to God the rules you have been holding onto. Honestly search your heart and ask the Spirit to reveal your motivations in even your most "Christian" behavior. Thank and praise God for the gift of Jesus Christ, who has freed you from the burden of achieving righteousness on your own. Ask God for help viewing your life as no longer belonging to you, but instead the property of Jesus Christ. Ask for fear to be cast out and for a sense of peace in God's salvation — over and beyond anything your efforts could achieve — to flood over you.

LIVE

The life you are living today is no longer your own. Christ lives in you, and his righteousness is what gives you confidence. Set aside your own confidence and live by faith in the Son of God alone today.

RIVERS OF LIGHT

JAMES 1:13-18

13-15   Don't let anyone under pressure to give in to evil say, "God is trying to trip me up." God is impervious to evil, and puts evil in no one's way. The temptation to give in to evil comes from us and only us. We have no one to blame but the leering, seducing flare-up of our own lust. Lust gets pregnant, and has a baby: sin! Sin grows up to adulthood, and becomes a real killer.

16-18   So, my very dear friends, don't get thrown off course. Every desirable and beneficial gift comes out of heaven. The gifts are rivers of light cascading down from the Father of Light. There is nothing deceitful in God, nothing two-faced, nothing fickle. He brought us to life using the true Word, showing us off as the crown of all his creatures.

READ

Read the passage through with an open heart to what God is saying to *you*.

THINK

In a world full of evil deeds and tough situations, it is very tempting to blame not only external circumstances but even sometimes God himself. If God is in charge, how can he possibly allow such things to happen and expect you to respond well? (Blame-shifting is one of the oldest human tendencies in a fallen world. See Genesis 2.) While James is *not* encouraging you to assume bad circumstances are your fault (this can be very dangerous), he *does* want to point out one simple truth: there is not a single evil intention or thought in the mind of God. God is the opposite of evil. You don't have to brace yourself for manipulation or abandonment from God. Instead, everything you get from him is "desirable and beneficial."

PRAY

Ask the Spirit to guide you in searching your heart. Don't be afraid of ugliness you might find — surrender sins up to God as they are unveiled to you. Be honest with God about your tough situations. Thank and praise God for his character of pure goodness and for his showering of good gifts upon you.

LIVE

Today you will be tempted by the evil within your own soul, disguised as outside factors or the fault of someone else. But God has given a power of goodness within you that is far stronger than the evil of your "old self." Concentrate on God's unchanging, pure goodness no matter what evil seems to come your way.

THE WORST IS NEVER THE WORST

LAMENTATIONS 3:25-33

25-27   GOD proves to be good to the man who passionately waits,
      to the woman who diligently seeks.
It's a good thing to quietly hope,
      quietly hope for help from GOD.
It's a good thing when you're young
      to stick it out through the hard times.

28-30   When life is heavy and hard to take,
      go off by yourself. Enter the silence.
Bow in prayer. Don't ask questions:
      Wait for hope to appear.
Don't run from trouble. Take it full-face.
      The "worst" is never the worst.

31-33   Why? Because the Master won't ever
      walk out and fail to return.
If he works severely, he also works tenderly.
      His stockpiles of loyal love are immense.
He takes no pleasure in making life hard,
      In throwing roadblocks in the way.

READ

As you read, consider that Jeremiah was not just writing about sorrow — he was experiencing it firsthand.

THINK

The man who passionately waits and the woman who diligently seeks are not representing different actions for different genders, but rather representing poetic parallels of one another. Hoping and waiting often go together, but somehow waiting can feel suspiciously passive to us. Why should we wait on God in hard times? What attitude should we maintain while waiting?

PRAY

Thank God for his unchanging and unfailing love. He is the Master who never fails to return. He takes no delight in making life difficult. Praise Christ for coming to experience sorrow alongside you and for taking on your burdens firsthand. Ask for the patience and strength to wait in hope. Express your worries and heartbrokenness directly to him, and pray for endurance and certainty in God's purposes.

LIVE

This author refers to God as the Master who won't fail to return. What other phrases can you come up with that describe God's faithfulness even in the midst of our fears?

_____

_____

_____

THE VOICE OF TRUTH

JOHN 18:36-38

36   "My kingdom," said Jesus, "doesn't consist of what you see around you. If it did, my followers would fight so that I wouldn't be handed over to the Jews. But I'm not that kind of king, not the world's kind of king."

37   Then Pilate said, "So, are you a king or not?"

Jesus answered, "You tell me. Because I am King, I was born and entered the world so that I could witness to the truth. Everyone who cares for truth, who has any feeling for the truth, recognizes my voice."

38   Pilate said, "What is truth?"

READ

Read the passage slowly, trying to imagine the scene — the sights, sounds, and emotions of both characters.

THINK

Jesus stands on trial before the Roman authority who has the power to clear or condemn. Jesus claims that if he were a king like others — if his kingdom were more related to "what you see around you," his followers would fight on his behalf. By comparison, what is the kingdom of God that Jesus rules over? What is it about the type of king Christ is that caused his rejection and arrest? How is the kingship of Jesus related to the truth? Is Jesus the king in your life?

PRAY

Praise God for Christ's unique servant-kingship and for his kingdom built on love, forgiveness, and truth. Be honest with God about where you see yourself in this story — whether it is as a doubter, a rejecter, or a believer. Ask God for the ability to recognize the voice of the truth in your life and in your heart.

LIVE

Recognizing the voice of Christ does not just refer to the literal words spoken in his time on earth. It means his continuing, ongoing work, which is happening through his church and through *you*. The truth is constantly speaking to you and calling to you. Listen to it today, even if you hear it in the most ordinary of places.

RECKLESS IN LOVE

JOHN 12:24-28

24-25   Listen carefully: Unless a grain of wheat is buried in the ground, dead to the world, it is never any more than a grain of wheat. But if it is buried, it sprouts and reproduces itself many times over. In the same way, anyone who holds on to life just as it is destroys that life. But if you let it go, reckless in your love, you'll have it forever, real and eternal.

26   If any of you wants to serve me, then follow me. Then you'll be where I am, ready to serve at a moment's notice. The Father will honor and reward anyone who serves me.

27-28   Right now I am storm-tossed. And what am I going to say? "Father, get me out of this"? No, this is why I came in the first place. I'll say, "Father, put your glory on display."

READ

Jesus tells his disciples to listen carefully — so read slowly and take it all in.

THINK

This is Jesus speaking to his disciples just before Judas betrays him. True to his teaching style, Jesus uses a metaphor to help his disciples "get the picture" from the world around them. Think about pruning roses, controlling forest fires, letting herbs go to seed, using fertilizer. Sometimes, trying to artificially avoid death actually prevents fruitful life. Gardeners know that death provides essential preparation for life to truly thrive. As Jesus faces his suffering and death, he doesn't simply accept it, he models letting go for all of those who follow him as a way to truly receive joy and life. Jesus trusts that whatever he gives away will come back to him a hundredfold — that the purpose of humanity is loving recklessly in full trust and abandonment to the will of God. What is your attitude toward death and suffering, both literal and spiritual? Do you shrink from it in dread and fear? Or do you believe that it will produce life and fruitfulness in you? What are you afraid of losing?

PRAY

Spend some time taking inventory of the things in your life you are most afraid to lose. Whether it is something as simple as time or something as complex as an unhealthy yet familiar relationship, you have something that you want to keep "above the ground" and outside of God's reach (if you could). Confess to God your fears and honestly release them to him. Ask for "reckless love" that isn't concerned about counting losses.

LIVE

You might not be able to change your whole life today, but you can drop a single "kernel of wheat" into the ground. What will you give away to make room for new and more abundant life?

44

YOU WERE KNOWN

ISAIAH 49:15-16

15-16   Can a mother forget the infant at her breast,
        walk away from the baby she bore?
    But even if mothers forget,
        I'd never forget you — never.
    Look, I've written your names on the backs of my hands.
        The walls you're rebuilding are never out of my sight.

READ

As you read the words of God to his people, focus on the image of maternity in this passage.

THINK

The first question is so rhetorical it is almost painful. The point is, God's care for his children is even more profound than the care of a mother. Mothers might forget their children eventually, from the ills of dementia or brain trauma. They might have broken relationships or misunderstandings with their dear ones. As a mother, you will wound your children in some way; as a child, you have been wounded by your mother in some way. Yet God's memory is perfect, his relationship with us is flawless and his mercy infinite. What do you think it means that the God of the universe has written your name on the back of his hand? Or that the walls you are building are never out of his sight?

PRAY

Praise God for a loving relationship that surpasses even the doting of an earthly mother. He knows you completely, perfectly, and endlessly, without any limiting conditions or human flaws in the way. Ask God for the proper way to respond to such an unfathomable connection.

LIVE

If you are a mother, write about how you can lead your children through their relationship with you to depend even more deeply on God. If you are without children, consider how you can use God's comparisons to an earthly parent to help mend or strengthen your relationship with your own mother.

NEW CREATION, NEW RELATIONSHIPS

2 CORINTHIANS 5:14-19

14-15 Our firm decision is to work from this focused center: One man died for everyone. That puts everyone in the same boat. He included everyone in his death so that everyone could also be included in his life, a resurrection life, a far better life than people ever lived on their own.

16-19 Because of this decision we don't evaluate people by what they have or how they look. We looked at the Messiah that way once and got it all wrong, as you know. We certainly don't look at him that way anymore. Now we look inside, and what we see is that anyone united with the Messiah gets a fresh start, is created new. The old life is gone; a new life burgeons! Look at it! All this comes from the God who settled the relationship between us and him, and then called us to settle our relationships with each other.

READ

Read the passage carefully. What words, phrases, and images stand out to you? What seems to be the main emotion driving the passage?

THINK

Christ's death and resurrection changes everything. It heals humanity's relationship with God and makes all who seek Christ new in him. However, it doesn't stop there. God has then also "called us to settle our relationships with each other." Christ didn't sacrifice himself for you and then leave out that one person who gets on your nerves. He has called everyone to new life, to resurrection and a fresh start — not only with God, but with one another. What relationships in your life need to be "resurrected"? Who do you need to reevaluate with the eyes of God's grace and love?

PRAY

Praise and thank God for his restoration and resurrection. Ask him to continue restoring you to himself and making new all that is old and dark and ugly in your heart. Pray also for growth and change in the way you handle relationships. Ask for discernment and courage in pursuing restoration.

LIVE

Restoration means love and repentance, whether you are the wounded or the one who inflicted wounds. How will you seek resurrection in a relationship today, new or old?

GOD'S GOOD WORKS

PSALM 33:4-7

4-5   For GOD's Word is solid to the core;
       everything he makes is sound inside and out.
    He loves it when everything fits,
       when his world is in plumb-line true.
    Earth is drenched
       in GOD's affectionate satisfaction.

6-7   The skies were made by GOD's command;
       he breathed the word and the stars popped out.
    He scooped Sea into his jug,
       put Ocean in his keg.

READ

Read this passage aloud several times through. Imagine the vivid pictures painted by the poetry.

THINK

It is so easy to focus on the brokenness in our world and our lives. We are bombarded by stories and circumstances that demonstrate the need for a Savior and for hope beyond this life. In the midst of that, however, we often forget that God created the world and called it "good" — and beneath all of the brokenness is still a creation meant to glorify him. What a person produces and how they work can often tell us much of who they are. What do these descriptions of God's creations — whether the world or his Word — tell us about the character of God? What is the scope of God's power? What brings God joy? What do you think it means that God loves "when everything fits"? Does it mean he has a bent for tidiness or something much more profound and beautiful?

PRAY

Praise God for his good creation. Whether it is the plants outside of your window, the peace of your home, or the security of your job, he has designed all things in this wide world with tender affection and ultimate power. Thank God for his workmanship.

LIVE

God delights when things are balanced and true, but the world is still fallen and weary. Cling to the thought that God's ultimate creation plan is good, ordered, and pointing to glory — no matter how busy your today or tomorrow is.

GENEROUSLY AND GRACIOUSLY

LUKE 6:35-38

35-36 I tell you, love your enemies. Help and give without expecting a return. You'll never—I promise—regret it. Live out this God-created identity the way our Father lives toward us, generously and graciously, even when we're at our worst. Our Father is kind; you be kind.

37-38 Don't pick on people, jump on their failures, criticize their faults—unless, of course, you want the same treatment. Don't condemn those who are down; that hardness can boomerang. Be easy on people; you'll find life a lot easier. Give away your life; you'll find life given back, but not merely given back—given back with bonus and blessing. Giving, not getting, is the way. Generosity begets generosity.

READ

Read this passage carefully and deeply. Don't turn off your brain once you hit that first familiar phrase. Approach the text to discover the meaning instead of assuming you've got it down.

THINK

This text does not mean you cannot communicate honestly to others. Don't think that love means you should enable sin. Look specifically at the verbs used in this translation that follow the "don't" command. "Pick on," "jump on," "criticize," "condemn" — what do they say about motivation? What is the command that Jesus is giving, assuming he doesn't want a bunch of "nice" but fake followers? "Enemies" often seem like the stuff of either comic books or petty fights, but Jesus was talking to all of us. Who are the "enemies" in your life and why? What does the love of the Father have to do with how you view them and how you treat them? How has God treated you?

PRAY

This is a tough one. Ask God to help you identify the "enemies" of your heart, even if it is a deeply hidden grudge or a casual and familiar hostility. Praise God for revealing his great grace even when we were his enemies. Ask for an understanding of the gospel so powerful and strong it will over-flow into your interactions with those who are your own enemies.

LIVE

Loving your enemies isn't a vague idea — it's a place of being that is going to be made up of concrete actions. How will you love your enemies today?

LET GOD-LIGHT WORK

JOHN 3:19-21

19-21   This is the crisis we're in: God-light streamed into the world, but men and women everywhere ran for the darkness. They went for the darkness because they were not really interested in pleasing God. Everyone who makes a practice of doing evil, addicted to denial and illusion, hates God-light and won't come near it, fearing a painful exposure. But anyone working and living in truth and reality welcomes God-light so the work can be seen for the God-work it is.

READ

The speaker in the passage is Jesus himself. Allow the words to wash over you.

THINK

Darkness automatically calls to mind weariness, fear, and danger. So why do men and women run toward the metaphorical darkness in this passage? Look at the vivid motivations that follow—addiction, hate, and fear show that sin is more powerful, potent, and persuasive than simply a less-than-perfect deed. In what ways is sin evasion? What do you think it means that when you seek darkness, you are "fearing a painful exposure"? Why and how do denial and illusion belong to the category of sin? God-light—God's work—is powerful and able to reveal to us and to those around us our fears and failures. It seems logical to run away. So how can we counter our insecurities? What does it mean to welcome God's light and reality into our lives even if it means "painful exposure"? Consider the famous words of John 3:16, which come just before this passage.

PRAY

Confess to God the painful exposure that you fear. Whether it is hidden sins or simply a habit you don't want to change, ask the Spirit to give you the truth of God's reality that will shed light and love. Thank and praise him for placing you in the truth and in the center of his work. Ask him for a sense of certainty in his saving love which helps us conquer the darkness—within and without.

LIVE

If God's light and reality expose the darkness within us, that also means it is available to provide us with truth. It can help us battle the illusions of the world. How will you bring God-light into your relationships? Into your family? Into your work?

TOOLS OF THE TRUTH

2 CORINTHIANS 10:3-6

3-6   The world is unprincipled. It's dog-eat-dog out there! The world doesn't fight fair. But we don't live or fight our battles that way — never have and never will. The tools of our trade aren't for marketing or manipulation, but they are for demolishing that entire massively corrupt culture. We use our powerful God-tools for smashing warped philosophies, tearing down barriers erected against the truth of God, fitting every loose thought and emotion and impulse into the structure of life shaped by Christ. Our tools are ready at hand for clearing the ground of every obstruction and building lives of obedience into maturity.

READ

Enter into the visuals provided by this passage. Try to pick out the key phrases.

THINK

In what ways are demolition and construction an appropriate metaphor for God's kingdom? What are some of the "warped philosophies" and "barriers erected against the truth of God" in our "massively corrupt culture"? Paul compares and contrasts the way the world uses destructive forces with the way we use our "God-tools." While the world seeks to destroy for the sake of survival or self-benefit, we do not seek to destroy others but only the forces of evil that try to mask the truth. How do you think this happens? What do you think the "God-tools" are? Is it primarily external or does this demolition also need to happen within you?

PRAY

Ask God to direct his powerful tools at your own heart, where warped philosophies and corrupt cultural norms have taken root. Pray for the revelation of truth and for every thought to become captive to Christ, who is building up a good work in this dark world.

LIVE

It's a "dog-eat-dog" world, but you are called to something so much bigger and more beautiful. Use the tools of the truth — including love — to battle the destructive forces at work in the world.

DIRECTED BY GOD

EXODUS 17:1-6

1-2 Directed by GOD, the whole company of Israel moved on by stages from the Wilderness of Sin. They set camp at Rephidim. And there wasn't a drop of water for the people to drink. The people took Moses to task: "Give us water to drink." But Moses said, "Why pester me? Why are you testing GOD?"

3 But the people were thirsty for water there. They complained to Moses, "Why did you take us from Egypt and drag us out here with our children and animals to die of thirst?"

4 Moses cried out in prayer to GOD, "What can I do with these people? Any minute now they'll kill me!"

5-6 GOD said to Moses, "Go on out ahead of the people, taking with you some of the elders of Israel. Take the staff you used to strike the Nile. And go. I'm going to be present before you there on the rock at Horeb. You are to strike the rock. Water will gush out of it and the people will drink."

READ

Set the scene in your imagination. As you read, consider the various emotions on both sides. It's easy to fixate on the Israelites' melodramatic complaints, but remember you might not sound so different.

THINK

Note carefully the phrase this whole survival scene starts with. *Would God really lead them where they could not live?* What are the various aspects of frustration in this passage and what is causing it? The people turn to Moses, afraid of their need, ready to kill perhaps because of their fear. Why does Moses balk at their questions? Do you often want answers from "the person in charge" instead of first turning to God? Do you ever take people to task in fear or anger? Moses turns directly to God, though perhaps with the same basic concern — self-preservation. The people he is leading are quickly turning into a mob who want instant gratification more than guidance. Does that "turned-upon" and harried feeling seem familiar to you?

PRAY

Identify yourself with the mistrust and complaints of the Israelites or the frustration and burden of Moses — or both. Tell God what it is that you feel you *need* to survive, and confess your fears about receiving it. Ask God directly for his miraculous provision and for the peace to trust him even in the wilderness.

LIVE

Write about the "wilderness" you are currently facing and the "water" you are afraid will not come. Instead of demanding it of God, see if you can identify places where he has already provided good things from unexpected places.

_____

_____

_____

CHRIST DISPLACES WORRY

PHILIPPIANS 4:6-7

6-7 Don't fret or worry. Instead of worrying, pray. Let petitions and praises shape your worries into prayers, letting God know your concerns. Before you know it, a sense of God's wholeness, everything coming together for good, will come and settle you down. It's wonderful what happens when Christ displaces worry at the center of your life.

READ

Read the passage slowly and carefully.

THINK

Praises and petitions can shape worries into prayers. Think about what causes you worry — whether your own actions, the actions of others, or simply circumstances that seem out of control. How could a "sense of God's wholeness" and "everything coming together for good" be a helpful thought to cling to? It is tempting, even culturally acceptable, to be worried, busy, anxious in the name of "productivity." But God never stops — he never gets tired. His work doesn't depend on your anxiety.

PRAY

Come clean about the worries that seem to be at the center of your life. Confess to Jesus your deep-seated fear of letting go, the feeling that if you do things will fall apart. Then practice what this passage says — praise and thank him for all of the great things he has done and for his promise to work all things together for good. Ask for a sense of trust in his wholeness, no matter what is coming your way.

LIVE

Think about your biggest anxiety trigger in your daily life and actions. Journal a prayer of thanksgiving to reflect on during that time.

_____

_____

_____

GOD'S CHILDREN

HOSEA 11:1-4

1-4   When Israel was only a child, I loved him.
     I called out, "My son!" — called him out of Egypt.
But when others called him,
     he ran off and left me.
He worshiped the popular sex gods,
     he played at religion with toy gods.
Still, I stuck with him. I led Ephraim.
     I rescued him from human bondage,
But he never acknowledged my help,
     never admitted that I was the one pulling his wagon,
That I lifted him, like a baby, to my cheek,
     that I bent down to feed him.

READ

Consider the image of mother and child. Read this passage carefully, attentive to the tone.

THINK

If you are a mother, write about how you might feel if your child at a young age wandered off or ran away, refusing your desperately needed help. If you are not a mother, reflect on a time when you or someone near you rebelled to hurt and wound the parent. Write about the connection between these very human emotions and God's feelings toward his children.

_____

_____

_____

PRAY

Ask God, your heavenly parent, for forgiveness. Thank him for his constant support and for caring for your every need. Praise him for always wanting to embrace you once again, even when you wander far without good reason. Pray for the ability to rest in his love and to become comfortable and consistent in dependence on him.

LIVE

Don't forget that you are God's child. Sin and selfish living aren't just a matter of breaking abstract rules like a traffic law, but rebellion against a real, loving, living person. Live carefully out of love for your heavenly Father.

SPREADING SALVATION

ISAIAH 49:4-6

4   I said, "I've worked for nothing.
        I've nothing to show for a life of hard work.
    Nevertheless, I'll let GOD have the last word.
        I'll let him pronounce his verdict."

5-6   "And now," GOD says,
        this God who took me in hand
        from the moment of birth to be his servant,
    To bring Jacob back home to him,
        to set a reunion for Israel —
    What an honor for me in GOD's eyes!
        That God should be my strength!
    He says, "But that's not a big enough job for my servant —
        just to recover the tribes of Jacob,
        merely to round up the strays of Israel.
    I'm setting you up as a light for the *nations*
        So that my salvation becomes *global*!"

READ

Read this passage aloud slowly. Don't worry about puzzling out the context right away — try to understand the sense of the passage simply by receiving and observing what is there.

THINK

This passage includes the perspective of the "Servant of God's" mission. These portions of Isaiah are usually interpreted as prophecies of the Messiah. The Servant's mission of reuniting, restoring, and redeeming Israel is relevant to the exiled audience of the time and also to the broader future of humanity's relationship with God. Yet, what do you see from the perspective of this mighty Servant as he thinks on his own work? Anyone chosen by God might often feel like the things they are doing are not effective. We know that Jesus' mission — to die a shameful death on a cross after summoning sinners and lowlifes to follow — seemed like foolishness to religious people and pagans alike. Yet where does the Servant of God place his trust? How does your service to God compare to this? Note God's response to what seems like an ineffective ministry — not only is he going to use what feels "in vain" to do something big, he is going to make it even bigger. God is in the business of generosity, not wasting time.

PRAY

Confess to God any weariness you feel in his service or fears you have that your labors are in vain. Submit your service to God, no matter how big or small, and ask for eyes to see the bigger work of redemption in place.

LIVE

Remember that even when your work feels pointless, if it is done in service to God it is of infinite value — much more value than you might think.

EXPANDED PASSAGE: 1 TIMOTHY 2

PRAY EVERY WAY YOU KNOW HOW

1 TIMOTHY 2:1-3

1-3 The first thing I want you to do is pray. Pray every way you know how, for everyone you know. Pray especially for rulers and their governments to rule well so we can be quietly about our business of living simply, in humble contemplation. This is the way our Savior God wants us to live.

READ

Read the passage slowly, allowing each phrase to sink in. Read the passage aloud again.

THINK

Prayer might seem like an obvious command, but why are we asked to do it? Note especially the cause and effect when you choose to pray for your rulers (anyone from a boss to a government). Is prayer your first response to those in power? Or is it complaint, plotting about what you could do better, anxiety about their power, the urge to flatter and please? What is the "so that" counterpart to praying for those in authority? What do you think it means to "live simply" in "humble contemplation"? Does that mean retreat from the world, or does it refer to a sort of attitude in the midst of the world? How does prayer allow you to live the way Jesus wants you to live?

PRAY

Spend time in prayer especially for those in authority, whether in the far-distant government or in the close-reaching space of your work. Pray not only for them but for the relationships of those Sin and selfish living aren't just a matter of breaking abstract rules like a traffic law, they lead, including yourself. Ask for the things you know that God wants of them, and humbly ask for guidance in your intercessions.

LIVE

God is the one who places all people into their realms of power. With this in mind, go about today prayerfully instead of anxiously or resentfully. God is all-powerful. Your only "job" is to live humbly as Christ wants of you.

CHEERFUL NO MATTER WHAT

1 THESSALONIANS 5:16-18

16-18   Be cheerful no matter what; pray all the time; thank God no matter what happens. This is the way God wants you who belong to Christ Jesus to live.

READ

Read this short but packed passage several times through. Try to discern the relationship of each of these commandments to one another.

THINK

Paul does not provide a list of things to do without reminding you of the source of that power: your identity. You *belong* to Christ Jesus. Your position as a child of God and as a follower of Jesus means that you live differently — not because you must, but because it flows out of your redeemed and renewed heart. In this world of many troubles, how can you be cheerful no matter what? Why must you pray all the time? How does that relate back to who you are?

PRAY

Pray for your prayer life. Confess to God what hinders you from praying often, what struggles you find when you come to prayer. Ask God for a heart of gratitude that helps to hold you steady no matter the circumstances.

LIVE

Remember that being cheerful does not have to mean false optimism or pretending like all is well. You have real reason for cheer and optimism that goes deeper than your present trouble. You belong to God — and God will win the battle.

BASIC AS BREAD

JOHN 6:35-40

35-38   Jesus said, "I am the Bread of Life. The person who aligns with me hungers no more and thirsts no more, ever. I have told you this explicitly because even though you have seen me in action, you don't really believe me. Every person the Father gives me eventually comes running to me. And once that person is with me, I hold on and don't let go. I came down from heaven not to follow my own whim but to accomplish the will of the One who sent me.

39-40   "This, in a nutshell, is that will: that everything handed over to me by the Father be completed — not a single detail missed — and at the wrap-up of time I have everything and everyone put together, upright and whole. This is what my Father wants: that anyone who sees the Son and trusts who he is and what he does and then aligns with him will enter *real* life, *eternal* life. My part is to put them on their feet alive and whole at the completion of time."

READ

Read the passage aloud slowly.

THINK

Consider all the ramifications of Jesus calling himself the "Bread of Life." Though our culture might have made you wary of carbohydrates, bread did not mean empty or unnecessary calories in Jesus' time. Of all of the food that Jesus could have used as a metaphor, he chose bread — simple, unpretentious, absolutely necessary. Jesus claims that although he is essential, there is still plenty of unbelief. What seems to be Jesus' role in salvation and "soul nutrition" compared to yours?

PRAY

Tell the Lord about your needs, physical, spiritual, and emotional, and even your unbelief and lack of trust. Ask Jesus to give you the ability to run toward him and embrace the salvation that *he* accomplishes for you.

LIVE

Today, when you physically hunger and thirst, think about God, who satisfies all of your deepest, most essential needs, and thank him for the reminder of his work.

GOD'S PLAN

JEREMIAH 29:4-7,10-11

4   This is the Message from GOD-of-the-Angel-Armies, Israel's God, to all the exiles I've taken from Jerusalem to Babylon:

5   "Build houses and make yourselves at home.

      "Put in gardens and eat what grows in that country.

6   "Marry and have children. Encourage your children to marry and have children so that you'll thrive in that country and not waste away.

7   "Make yourselves at home there and work for the country's welfare.

      "Pray for Babylon's well-being. If things go well for Babylon, things will go well for you." . . .

10-11   This is GOD's Word on the subject: "As soon as Babylon's seventy years are up and not a day before, I'll show up and take care of you as I promised and bring you back home. I know what I'm doing. I have it all planned out — plans to take care of you, not abandon you, plans to give you the future you hope for."

READ

Read the passage through slowly, considering the full message.

THINK

God is speaking to the Israelites who have just been taken into captivity—and who are being commanded not to rebel, but to make the best of the situation. In fact, they are told to pray for the welfare of their enemies who hold them captive—the immoral, godless pagans who have destroyed their nation. This is the context for the often quoted verse 11, which promises God's plan and future hope. How do you reconcile prosperity and exile? Those two ideas seem contradictory, and yet they are both present in the text. Has God's plan in your life ever seemed to include exile, loss, and loneliness?

PRAY

Ask God to reveal to you the places of "exile" in your life—difficult relationships or situations that he has called you to thrive in. Pray for the welfare of those who cause you trouble or less-than-ideal circumstances, and ask for the ways in which you can prosper and "settle in," even if it feels foreign and counterintuitive. Request to envision the prosperity God gives, both immediately and long-term. Hope.

LIVE

The wonderful thing about this passage is that it promises tough times are not a sign of God's abandonment. Look ahead. Refuse to get discouraged. God has it all planned out.

PLANS FOR YOUR GOOD

GENESIS 50:16-21

16-17 They sent Joseph a message, "Before his death, your father gave this command: Tell Joseph, 'Forgive your brothers' sin — all that wrongdoing. They did treat you very badly.' Will you do it? Will you forgive the sins of the servants of your father's God?"

When Joseph received their message, he wept.

18 Then the brothers went in person to him, threw themselves on the ground before him and said, "We'll be your slaves."

19-21 Joseph replied, "Don't be afraid. Do I act for God? Don't you see, you planned evil against me but God used those same plans for my good, as you see all around you right now — life for many people. Easy now, you have nothing to fear; I'll take care of you and your children." He reassured them, speaking with them heart-to-heart.

READ

Read the passage slowly, entering into the emotions on all sides. Imagine the scene.

THINK

Look at the way that Joseph's brothers approach him for forgiveness. They do not even begin with their own apology — they relate the request of their father for their forgiveness before even venturing to ask for it themselves. They refer to themselves not as his brothers, but as "the servants of your father's God." They throw themselves onto the ground before they look into his face. How is it that Joseph is able to forgive them? Consider how God took man's evil plans and not only transformed them into working for Joseph's good, but for the good of many others who would be touched by Joseph's behavior of integrity in a "bad" situation. What does this show you about the way God works as opposed to the way humans work?

PRAY

You are in need of forgiveness and in need of forgiving others. Praise God for his incredible sovereignty that can work even your wounds into a plan of goodness. Ask him to open your eyes to the great things he has worked through brokenness in your past. Ask for forgiveness and a heart of generosity toward those who have wronged you and also for the courage to honestly approach those you have sinned against. Thank God for his grace, which allows you to be gracious without fear.

LIVE

No matter what man intends for evil, God can and will use it for the good of those who love him. Live today in forgiveness, trusting that God redeems even the worst of intentions, including your own.

THE BATTLE BELONGS TO GOD

1 SAMUEL 17:44-49

44   "Come on," said the Philistine. "I'll make roadkill of you for the buzzards. I'll turn you into a tasty morsel for the field mice."

45-47   David answered, "You come at me with sword and spear and battle-ax. I come at you in the name of God-of-the-Angel-Armies, the God of Israel's troops, whom you curse and mock. This very day God is handing you over to me. I'm about to kill you, cut off your head, and serve up your body and the bodies of your Philistine buddies to the crows and coyotes. The whole earth will know that there's an extraordinary God in Israel. And everyone gathered here will learn that God doesn't save by means of sword or spear. The battle belongs to God — he's handing you to us on a platter!"

48-49   That roused the Philistine, and he started toward David. David took off from the front line, running toward the Philistine. David reached into his pocket for a stone, slung it, and hit the Philistine hard in the forehead, embedding the stone deeply. The Philistine crashed, facedown in the dirt.

READ

Savor this climactic moment as if for the first time as you read the passage through.

THINK

The story of David and Goliath has become so familiar that the very phrase is a stand-in for any little-versus-big story. Is there more to this story than size, however? What truths do you notice hidden in David's speech to Goliath? In your own life, you might not have enemies literally drawing battle lines and taunting you with failure. If you did, maybe it would be easier to know what direction to charge in. What battles and enemies *are* in your life? What threats do they make against the quality of your life, if not your life itself? Look again at David's responses. What truths can you use to ground you in the certainty of faith in any battle?

PRAY

Identify the battles that seem the biggest in your life right now, the looming giants that seem certain to crush and destroy. Confess to God your anxieties and fears. Thank God that the battle truly belongs to him and that he is powerful beyond your abilities. Ask God for wisdom and discernment in how to "arm" yourself against these battles.

LIVE

How will you choose to live out the truth that "the battle belongs to GOD" today?

GOD'S NOBODIES

1 CORINTHIANS 1:25-31

25 Human wisdom is so tinny, so impotent, next to the seeming absurdity of God. Human strength can't begin to compete with God's "weakness."

26-31 Take a good look, friends, at who you were when you got called into this life. I don't see many of "the brightest and the best" among you, not many influential, not many from high-society families. Isn't it obvious that God deliberately chose men and women that the culture overlooks and exploits and abuses, chose these "nobodies" to expose the hollow pretensions of the "somebodies"? That makes it quite clear that none of you can get by with blowing your own horn before God. Everything that we have — right thinking and right living, a clean slate and a fresh start — comes from God by way of Jesus Christ. That's why we have the saying, "If you're going to blow a horn, blow a trumpet for God."

READ

Read the passage aloud to yourself slowly, allowing each phrase to sink in.

THINK

Start thinking about God's chosen ones in the Old Testament and all the way into the present age. Why do you think God prefers "nobodies" for his work? If God chooses nobodies, and he has chosen *you*, how should this truth color your daily actions, success and failure alike? Remember that the ultimate success of God — the death and resurrection of Jesus Christ — appeared like an incredible failure until its completion. What light does that truth cast on your own circumstances, good and bad?

PRAY

Confess to God the "human wisdom" that seems to hold you back from true humility and submission. Whether it is financial "common sense" or "normal" risk-taking, bring it before God and ask for true discernment and true heavenly wisdom. Ask God for a revelation of his "weakness" and for the courage to enter into it. Ask God for the strength to pick up the cross, however that might appear to those around you.

LIVE

What will change about your daily activities with the knowledge that God's "weakness" and God's "nobodies" matter far more from those who are successful and strong? Reflect the upside-down politics of the gospel wherever you go today.

A TRUTHFUL WITNESS

MARK 16:9-16

9-11   After rising from the dead, Jesus appeared early on Sunday morning to Mary Magdalene, whom he had delivered from seven demons. She went to his former companions, now weeping and carrying on, and told them. When they heard her report that she had seen him alive and well, they didn't believe her.

12-13   Later he appeared, but in a different form, to two of them out walking in the countryside. They went back and told the rest, but they weren't believed either.

14-16   Still later, as the Eleven were eating supper, he appeared and took them to task most severely for their stubborn unbelief, refusing to believe those who had seen him raised up. Then he said, "Go into the world. Go everywhere and announce the Message of God's good news to one and all. Whoever believes and is baptized is saved; whoever refuses to believe is damned."

READ

Read the passage slowly and carefully. Imagine the setting. Imagine the emotions of the various people involved.

THINK

Jesus appeared first to the one who had the least social status, the least credibility as a witness — he appeared to a woman. Mary was overwhelmed and overcome, and by the description of the Scriptures, not really in any fit state to go anywhere. And yet, without being instructed, she went and told the others. She *had* to tell the others. Although they did not believe her at first, the truthfulness of her witness was later validated by Jesus himself. Have you ever had the painful experience of not being believed, or being rejected as an exaggerator? It's so difficult that often we would rather not speak what we are seeing at all than risk scorn. Do you have the courage to speak anyway and witness to a skeptical world about Jesus' work in your life?

PRAY

Ask God for the courage to speak what you see without anxiety over what others might think of you. Ask also for a strength of spirit that makes your words appealing and a beauty of life that causes others to ask for your testimony.

LIVE

Write down the risks you face in sharing the truth about Christ with others. Also write down the potential benefits.

_____

_____

_____

WADE RIGHT IN

ROMANS 15:3-6

3-6 That's exactly what Jesus did. He didn't make it easy for himself by avoiding people's troubles, but waded right in and helped out. "I took on the troubles of the troubled," is the way Scripture puts it. Even if it was written in Scripture long ago, you can be sure it's written for *us*. God wants the combination of his steady, constant calling and warm, personal counsel in Scripture to come to characterize *us*, keeping us alert for whatever he will do next. May our dependably steady and warmly personal God develop maturity in you so that you get along with each other as well as Jesus gets along with us all. Then we'll be a choir — not our voices only, but our very lives singing in harmony in a stunning anthem to the God and Father of our Master Jesus!

READ

Read the passage through slowly and carefully. Observe the phrases that stand out to you.

THINK

Paul holds up Jesus as an example of the way we should work with people in trouble: not avoiding them, but instead identifying with them. While we are not the Lord — able to save and to redeem — we can reach out with his love to those in need. When you are working with the troubled people in your life, how can you be compassionate, constant, and yet also completely trusting in God's work rather than your own good deeds?

PRAY

Ask for discernment to minister to those in trouble around you. Pray for guidance in how to love these people so that your relationships form a beautiful choir, glorifying God. Thank Jesus for his solidarity with you in your own troubles, which saves you from isolation even in your hardest times. Praise him for the gift of passing that comfort along to others.

LIVE

Troubles do not have to be big, crushing, obvious burdens. They might be the simple anxieties of those around you. Find a way to reach out to those you have prayed for. Imitate Jesus' love.

A SPACIOUS, FREE LIFE

ROMANS 8:5-8

5-8 Those who think they can do it on their own end up obsessed with measuring their own moral muscle but never get around to exercising it in real life. Those who trust God's action in them find that God's Spirit is in them—living and breathing God! Obsession with self in these matters is a dead end; attention to God leads us out into the open, into a spacious, free life. Focusing on the self is the opposite of focusing on God. Anyone completely absorbed in self ignores God, ends up thinking more about self than God. That person ignores who God is and what he is doing. And God isn't pleased at being ignored.

READ

Read the passage slowly and carefully, considering how each new idea connects to the one before it. Consider the main tone and message of this passage.

THINK

Is it possible to be spiritual and yet still self-centered? Perhaps you have had a bad run-in with someone exhibiting this contradiction, or perhaps you have seen its ugliness surfacing in your own heart. Sometimes the sin nature hijacks the Christian life and draws focus to self—about what you are doing well, or even latching onto shame that swallows you up and leaves you feeling without hope. Thinking about what to do, however, is a "dead end"—the same claustrophobic and closed-off feeling you had before Jesus. Focusing on God—what he does for you and in you—is freeing and is the ultimate act of glorifying him.

PRAY

Ask God for forgiveness from relying too much on yourself and your own "moral muscle." Confess your inability, and praise and thank him for his complete ability. Pray for rescue from self-centered spirituality and discernment to see its effects in your life. Ask the Spirit to help you avoid anything that is not complete dependence on God's work and goodness.

LIVE

Journal about where you see self-centered spirituality creeping into your life and how you will refocus to make God the center.

TAKE HEART!

ISAIAH 35:3-7

3-4
Energize the limp hands,
strengthen the rubbery knees.
Tell fearful souls,
"Courage! Take heart!
GOD is here, right here,
on his way to put things right
And redress all wrongs.
He's on his way! He'll save you!"

5-7
Blind eyes will be opened,
deaf ears unstopped,
Lame men and women will leap like deer,
the voiceless break into song.
Springs of water will burst out in the wilderness,
streams flow in the desert.
Hot sands will become a cool oasis,
thirsty ground a splashing fountain.
Even lowly jackals will have water to drink,
And barren grasslands flourish richly.

READ

Read the passage slowly, allowing the imagery to wash over you.

THINK

You might comfort a child by assuring them of your presence. Here God does essentially the same thing. Our hands are limp. Our knees are rubbery, then "GOD is here, right here." What is the purpose of courage and the reason to have courage in this passage? Review the list of events coinciding with God's arrival — how would you sum them up in a single word? Why do you think the images of redemption here are beyond simply a single, internal moment of decision? How does God makes things right?

PRAY

Ask God for a bigger, broader, and more beautiful view of his redemption — one that explodes out of church doors and Christian boxes and colors everything in the world around you. Thank God for his miraculous salvation and for his process of renewal that affects the entire universe. Ask God to make you a part of that renewing force as you work to further his kingdom.

LIVE

Come up with your own special metaphor of renewal which affects your daily life and world. Carry it around with you today as a private reminder of God's ability to redeem even the driest places.

LOVE BANISHES FEAR

1 JOHN 4:17-19

17-18   God is love. When we take up permanent residence in a life of love, we live in God and God lives in us. This way, love has the run of the house, becomes at home and mature in us, so that we're free of worry on Judgment Day — our standing in the world is identical with Christ's. There is no room in love for fear. Well-formed love banishes fear. Since fear is crippling, a fearful life — fear of death, fear of judgment — is one not yet fully formed in love.

19   We, though, are going to love — love and be loved. First we were loved, now we love. He loved us first.

READ

Read the passage through aloud. Pause. Read the passage through once more, slowly.

THINK

These words are so familiar they often get distilled into bumper sticker-like phrases in our minds. Phrases like "God is love" and "Perfect love casts out fear" might have become overly familiar, even worn out, to you. But why do you think fear must be discussed when love, particularly God's love, comes up? What is it that you fear most deeply in your life — in your job, in your relationships, and in your spiritual walk? Why and how might God's love change everything and leave absolutely no room for things that frighten you?

PRAY

Confess to God the things that frighten you most deeply — whether it relates to your walk with him or your shortcomings with others. Thank God for his love, which is constant, and for his gospel, which means that no matter what you have done, he views you as his own perfect child. Ask God for an understanding of what it means to live in love. Invite Jesus to change your patterns of fear into forward motion: receiving and giving divine love.

LIVE

Journal about the places where fear is trying to crowd out love.

DESIGNS FOR GLORIOUS LIVING

EPHESIANS 1:11-14

11-12   It's in Christ that we find out who we are and what we are living for. Long before we first heard of Christ and got our hopes up, he had his eye on us, had designs on us for glorious living, part of the overall purpose he is working out in everything and everyone.

13-14   It's in Christ that you, once you heard the truth and believed it (this Message of your salvation), found yourselves home free — signed, sealed, and delivered by the Holy Spirit. This signet from God is the first installment on what's coming, a reminder that we'll get everything God has planned for us, a praising and glorious life.

READ

Read the passage once through slowly. Pause. Read the passage aloud again.

THINK

Amazingly, this passage reveals God's designs and plans and your place in them. Based on what you know of God and the hope of the gospel, what do you think "everything God has planned" for you means in this life and in the next? In what way does Christ help you to define who you are and what you are living for? What is the "seal" of the Holy Spirit on your life that gives evidence to this promise — the way it is already at work and the way it will come to fruition?

PRAY

Thank God for his marvelous plans, which involved you before you could even be aware of him. Praise God for beginning a work in your life which he will faithfully complete. Ask him to help you live more fully in that identity. Ask God for the specific ways in which you can practice "glorious living" even while you still walk in this earthly place.

LIVE

Write down specific things in your life that reveal the mark and the work of the Spirit. Write the way you want to see "glorious living" increase as you trust in God's plan.

_____

_____

_____

YOUR JOB: TO BLESS

1 PETER 3:8-12

8-12 Summing up: Be agreeable, be sympathetic, be loving, be compassionate, be humble. That goes for all of you, no exceptions. No retaliation. No sharp-tongued sarcasm. Instead, bless — that's your job, to bless. You'll be a blessing and also get a blessing.

> Whoever wants to embrace life
>   and see the day fill up with good,
> Here's what you do:
>   Say nothing evil or hurtful;
> Snub evil and cultivate good;
>   run after peace for all you're worth.
> God looks on all this with approval,
>   Listening and responding well to what he's asked;
> But he turns his back
>   on those who do evil things.

READ

Read the passage slowly and carefully, considering each phrase.

THINK

Peter gives a seemingly tall order. To consider your "job" as blessing instead of competing with others is a completely different worldview in a culture fueled by aggression and "survival of the fittest" sarcasm. But the source of these actions is not your own strength. What does it mean to "run after peace for all you're worth"? What sort of peace do you need to chase in your community? Which of these commands is the hardest for you to obey? Consider that there might be someone specific you are called to simply bless in your community.

PRAY

Ask God to fill you with his Spirit, which makes it possible to pursue peace and blessing instead of poisonous ambition. Pray through each of these commands in turn, asking for God to show you the way toward greater sympathy, love, compassion, humility, and a more guarded tongue. Praise God for granting you supernatural help in developing worthy relationships and becoming a blessing to others.

LIVE

If blessing others is your "job description" in Jesus, consider that it's not just abstract well-wishing. What concrete actions do you need to undertake to bless others in your community today?

GOING THE WRONG DIRECTION

JONAH 1:1-5

1-2 One day long ago, GOD's Word came to Jonah, Amittai's son: "Up on your feet and on your way to the big city of Nineveh! Preach to them. They're in a bad way and I can't ignore it any longer."

3 But Jonah got up and went the other direction to Tarshish, running away from GOD. He went down to the port of Joppa and found a ship headed for Tarshish. He paid the fare and went on board, joining those going to Tarshish — as far away from GOD as he could get.

4-5 But GOD sent a huge storm at sea, the waves towering.

The ship was about to break into pieces. The sailors were terrified. They called out in desperation to their gods. They threw everything they were carrying overboard to lighten the ship. Meanwhile, Jonah had gone down into the hold of the ship to take a nap. He was sound asleep.

READ

Read the passage carefully and observantly. The first lines of any story generally set the tone for the whole.

THINK

This story is probably familiar to you, but try not to get distracted by the flannelgraph and goldfish crackers version. What fundamental action and reaction do you see in the opening lines of this story? Assuming that Jonah wasn't just fickle (which is a possibility), what are some of the reasons why he might have gone in the opposite direction of Nineveh? What sorts of things cause you to go away from the calling of God in your life? Fear? Confusion? Doubt? Laziness? A sense of entitlement?

PRAY

Confess to God where you are avoiding his call. Whether it is a relationship, task, or bad habit, be honest about what fears you have or what responsibilities you are trying to evade. Ask God to reveal his purposes in his calling and for the courage to be submissive to his will.

LIVE

What if today you stubbornly refuse to be stubborn? What if you set yourself to do exactly what you know God is calling you to do? Just try it!

PRAYER OVER PREENING

1 TIMOTHY 2:8-10

8-10   Since prayer is at the bottom of all this, what I want mostly is for men to pray — not shaking angry fists at enemies but raising holy hands to God. And I want women to get in there with the men in humility before God, not primping before a mirror or chasing the latest fashions but doing something beautiful for God and becoming beautiful doing it.

READ

Read the passage through slowly. Pause after each phrase and observe each facet of these commands.

THINK

Men shaking angry fists and women primping before the mirror seem like dreadful stereotypes. But isn't that what we become when our mind detaches from God and we lose our focus? Assume that looking nice is not inherently sinful. What is the bigger issue that Paul is pointing toward as a danger sign, specifically for women? What does it mean to become beautiful by "doing something beautiful for God"?

PRAY

Take honest stock before God of your view on beauty. No need to repent for makeup — however, do you truly trust God and the deeds of God to make you beautiful instead of your own efforts? Ask God for true discernment in how you use your time and how much control you allow image to have in your life. Confess to God the fear and insecurities that often drive your choices — both good and bad.

LIVE

Journal about your revelations regarding beauty, humility, and God-defined loveliness.

_____

_____

_____

THE KING IS WILD FOR YOU

PSALM 45:10-15

10-12   "Now listen, daughter, don't miss a word:
       forget your country, put your home behind you.
   Be *here* — the king is wild for you.
       Since he's your lord, adore him.
   Wedding gifts pour in from Tyre;
       rich guests shower you with presents."

13-15   (Her wedding dress is dazzling,
       lined with gold by the weavers;
   All her dresses and robes
       are woven with gold.
   She is led to the king,
       followed by her virgin companions.
   A procession of joy and laughter!
       a grand entrance to the king's palace!)

READ

Read the passage slowly, allowing all of the emotions and images to flood in.

THINK

Although this passage is not describing *your* wedding, believers are encouraged to see marriage as a symbol of the binding love that God (the bridegroom) has for his people — which means you. Think about weddings you have attended. Remember the look in the groom's face when he saw his bride? Remember the radiance of the woman in white? What comes to your mind when you hear the phrase "the king is wild for you"? Marriage is an incredibly apt symbol of God's grace; it is a celebration of love and being loved. On her wedding day, a bride is not beautiful because of her accomplishments or her family or any other identity that the world deems so important — she is basking in the joy of being sought out, pursued, and bound forever by one who loves her. If the King of All Creation seeks you out like that, what do you think is an appropriate response?

PRAY

Praise and thank God, the Bridegroom, for this image of love given to us. Ask him for a sense of his love and for a revelation of his work already in courting you. Ask for the joy of a marriage celebration as you contemplate the good news of the gospel and the great intentions of God's love.

LIVE

Live like a bride today. To your God, you are as beautiful, fresh, and beloved as the day a woman dons white. Celebrate the love you have! Be present to your groom!

LEADING IN PRAISE

EXODUS 15:19-21

19 Yes, Pharaoh's horses and chariots and riders went into the sea and GOD turned the waters back on them; but the Israelites walked on dry land right through the middle of the sea.

20-21 Miriam the prophetess, Aaron's sister, took a tambourine, and all the women followed her with tambourines, dancing. Miriam led them in singing,

> Sing to GOD —
> What a victory!
> He pitched horse and rider
> into the sea!

READ

Read the passage aloud slowly.

THINK

Moses has just led the Israelites across the Red Sea. Now Miriam is leading the Israelites in a powerful song. It might be tempting to imagine leadership as a somewhat solemn thing and leaders as those who help people through what *must* be done. But Miriam was a leader in joy. She led the singing and dancing in commemoration of God's great deed. Why do you think the author took pains to record Miriam's actions? What is important about her role in the community? Could being a leader in rejoicing be something that you are called to? What might that look like in your life? Assuming you don't need a tambourine, how might you be able to loudly model praise and thanksgiving?

PRAY

Thank God for the miracles he has worked in your life and in your community. Praise him for the deliverance he has brought about. Ask God for greater joy and greater thanksgiving — for gratitude so big you cannot help but lead others in the same contagious celebration of grace. Ask for creative ways to be a leader in your community, especially in places where you already have a position of authority.

LIVE

What is the greatest of God's deliverances in your life? Take a moment to creatively praise him for his mighty work.

DON'T WASTE YOUR TIME

EPHESIANS 5:11-16

11-16 Don't waste your time on useless work, mere busywork, the barren pursuits of darkness. Expose these things for the sham they are. It's a scandal when people waste their lives on things they must do in the darkness where no one will see. Rip the cover off those frauds and see how attractive they look in the light of Christ.

> Wake up from your sleep,
> Climb out of your coffins;
> Christ will show you the light!

So watch your step. Use your head. Make the most of every chance you get. These are desperate times!

READ

Read the passage slowly and observantly.

THINK

It might be tempting to think using time wisely means packing more in — being as busy as possible and feeling guilt for leisure. What is the difference between work that must be done and "mere busywork" and "useless work"? How does the gospel help you discern between frantic activity and fruitful obedience? Note the "pursuits of darkness" are barren — they bring nothing about. Why is it then so easy to pursue those things? Why do you think Paul is so urgent about timeliness? What does he mean by saying that "these are desperate times"?

PRAY

Daily tasks are not necessarily wastes of time, but sometimes your most "important" activities need to be surrendered to the light. Cry to God for deliverance from the barren pursuits of darkness. Bring your tasks and timing to the light of the Cross. Thank God for bringing the truth to the light.

LIVE

Journal about your biggest "busywork" barren pursuit so you can bring the light of Jesus into it.

_____

_____

_____

POTTER AND CLAY

ISAIAH 64:6-9

6-7   We're all sin-infected, sin-contaminated.
        Our best efforts are grease-stained rags.
    We dry up like autumn leaves —
        sin-dried, we're blown off by the wind.
    No one prays to you
        or makes the effort to reach out to you.
    Because you've turned away from us,
        left us to stew in our sins.

8-9   Still, GOD, you are our Father.
        We're the clay and you're our potter:
        All of us are what you made us.
    Don't be too angry with us, O GOD.
        Don't keep a permanent account of wrongdoing.
        Keep in mind, please, we *are* your people — all of us.

READ

Read the passage slowly, paying attention to the images and the details of the prophet's language. Reread the passage from the "still" portion onward.

THINK

Carefully consider the images in the first two verses and what they reveal about the nature of sin. Sin is infectious — contagious. It eats away at you like a disease and affects everything you do, sometimes before you even realize it. It is choice and yet it is also a condition — something you are born with, something you can make worse, something you hope to be rid of and yet can't escape. How does the author characterize our efforts to make things better? This view of sin is vital to understanding our position in contrast to God's grace.

PRAY

Spend time in confession before God, considering the way sin runs through your heart and your life. Whether you have been sinned against or you have sinned against others, ask God to reveal the corruption so that you can have a greater sense of his deliverance. Ask for forgiveness from your own efforts at cleaning up with grease-stained rags, and ask for the true cleansing forgiveness of Jesus' blood. Praise God that you are still his own dear child, bought with a price.

LIVE

Live today with a greater awareness of sin, in yourself and in the world around you. Instead of despairing when you see the spotted portions of your soul, turn purposefully to Jesus for help and remind yourself of his love.

WAIT WITH HOPE

PSALM 131:2-3

2   I've kept my feet on the ground,
        I've cultivated a quiet heart.
    Like a baby content in its mother's arms,
        my soul is a baby content.

3   Wait, Israel, for GOD. Wait with hope.
        Hope now; hope always!

READ

Call to mind holding a small, content infant in your arms. Read this passage aloud slowly, several times through.

THINK

Based on your experience, why are babies so content in their mothers' arms? What is present in their little souls and what is not when they are in that space? Answer with as much or as little physical detail as you like. How could the psalmist become like that in God's presence? How could you?

PRAY

Praise God for being nurturer, protector, and a faithful and present parent. God has never left you and will never leave you. God cares for you regardless of what you can and cannot do or what fuss you put up. Thank him for this incredible gift. Ask for God's presence and a sense of his identity to calm the anxious spirit within you and give way to hope.

LIVE

A child in their mother's arms has no sense of urgency, no need for accomplishment, and no frustration at their inability. They simply soak up the presence of the protecting, nurturing force that keeps them safe. No matter what comes your way today, remember that God holds you in his arms. You have no cause for fear.

OUR PAINS HE CARRIED

ISAIAH 53:4-6

4-6   The fact is, it was *our* pains he carried —
        our disfigurements, all the things wrong with *us*.
    We thought he brought it on himself,
        that God was punishing him for his own failures.
    But it was our sins that did that to him,
        that ripped and tore and crushed him — *our sins!*
    He took the punishment, and that made us whole.
        Through his bruises we get healed.
    We're all like sheep who've wandered off and gotten lost.
        We've all done our own thing, gone our own way.
    And GOD has piled all our sins, everything we've done wrong,
        on him, on him.

READ

Slowly read the passage aloud, pausing fully between sentences and phrases. Then read it through again silently.

THINK

The Servant of God, Jesus, took on all the things wrong and twisted in the world — all the things scarred and broken inside of *you*. Think about what weighs you down the most on sleepless nights and in lonely, frightened moments. The words you have regretted, the relationships you have lost or been wounded by, the lack of love you fear — all of those deep, dark things Jesus took upon himself. For what purpose? To make you whole and to heal you. God took upon himself all of the things that you build as barriers to his presence — all of the things that make you the most unfit for heaven. By taking them on, he allows you to be reunited with God, made perfect and shining, with your innocence restored. What does that mean for your sin, now, *today*?

PRAY

Thank God for his incredible act of sacrifice, for his love so great it took on your pain. Praise God for his gift of wholeness and healing. Ask for greater love, greater trust, and greater mercy as a response to this marvelous redemption.

LIVE

Jesus has taken all of your sins and made you free to live whole and healed before God. Live in that identity today instead of concerning yourself with old sins. His love wins.

GOD GETS
THE LAST WORD

1 PETER 5:8-11

8-11   Keep a cool head. Stay alert. The Devil is poised to pounce, and would like nothing better than to catch you napping. Keep your guard up. You're not the only ones plunged into these hard times. It's the same with Christians all over the world. So keep a firm grip on the faith. The suffering won't last forever. It won't be long before this generous God who has great plans for us in Christ — eternal and glorious plans they are! — will have you put together and on your feet for good. He gets the last word; yes, he does.

READ

Read the passage slowly.

THINK

Consider the difference between being "alert" and afraid or anxious. What sort of attitude does this suggest toward evil? While it is true that the battle ultimately belongs to God, what is your role in it? In addition to encouraging believers to keep their guards up, notice that Peter also mentions the suffering of believers in general. Why is it important to recognize that we are not the only ones who struggle and that the struggle is not the ultimate reality of our lives? What sort of "great plans" do you hope "this generous God" has for you?

PRAY

Praise God for already winning the battle between good and evil by defeating death, sin, and hell with his glorious resurrection. Ask God for wisdom when and where you are most vulnerable to being caught unaware by evil. Thank God for his good plans, and ask for courage in the midst of the temporary suffering you are experiencing.

LIVE

Record some practical things you can do today to "keep your guard up" against the Devil. How will you fill your heart and mind with God's plans so that you are not caught unaware?

_____

_____

_____

STRIVING VERSUS TRUST

GALATIANS 3:2-6

2-4   Let me put this question to you: How did your new life begin? Was it by working your heads off to please God? Or was it by responding to God's Message to you? Are you going to continue this craziness? For only crazy people would think they could complete by their own efforts what was begun by God. If you weren't smart enough or strong enough to begin it, how do you suppose you could perfect it? Did you go through this whole painful learning process for nothing? It is not yet a total loss, but it certainly will be if you keep this up!

5-6   Answer this question: Does the God who lavishly provides you with his own presence, his Holy Spirit, working things in your lives you could never do for yourselves, does he do these things because of your strenuous moral striving *or* because you trust him to do them in you? Don't these things happen among you just as they happened with Abraham? He believed God, and that act of belief was turned into a life that was right with God.

READ

Read the passage through. Try to imagine the tone of the communication.

THINK

God's work of salvation — for you and for the entire world — comes from the same source and power that created the universe. All God asks of you is trust and love. Why is it so easy to try to turn back to your own efforts? Why does control so often seem more appealing than surrender? Where do you see "striving" in your life at war with trust?

PRAY

Confess to God your own attempts at salvation. Lay before God all of the other things you have felt essential to your spiritual standing with him. Thank God for his work of salvation, which is begun and completed by him with more power and wisdom than you could ever muster on your own. Ask God for increased faith and trust — for a willingness to relinquish "strenuous moral striving" and instead have a spirit willing to freely accept Christ's righteousness.

LIVE

Journal about some ways in which your moral striving often gets in the way of God's free salvation. How will you pursue trust instead?

_____

_____

_____

MIND YOUR OWN BUSINESS

1 THESSALONIANS 4:11-12

11-12 Stay calm; mind your own business; do your own job. You've heard all this from us before, but a reminder never hurts. We want you living in a way that will command the respect of outsiders, not lying around sponging off your friends.

READ

Read the passage slowly and carefully, pausing to allow all of the words to take root in you.

THINK

Usually the connotations of the phrase "mind your own business" are negative—a response to someone who has butted in or a defensive cry from someone who does not want to share their life. Journal about what you think it means to "mind your own business" in tension with the call to compassionately carry the burdens of one another. How is this difficult, especially as a woman?

_____

_____

_____

PRAY

Ask God for the courage and strength to discern gossip and to resist it. Pray for the wisdom to know when to "mind your own business" and when to reach out—the fine line between caring, helping, and meddling is something that can only come from the Spirit. Examine before him the conversation you have with your fellow sisters in Christ and confess what is not Spirit-filled.

LIVE

As women, we are drawn to delve in and discuss all things deeply—sometimes we discuss the lives of others more than we reflect on our own depth and quality of life. Guard your speech carefully today—when you are tempted to discuss and analyze another woman, turn your curiosity on your own heart and mind instead, bringing it before the Lord.

AIMING TO BE NOBODY

ROMANS 12:14-21

14-16   Bless your enemies; no cursing under your breath. Laugh with your happy friends when they're happy; share tears when they're down. Get along with each other; don't be stuck-up. Make friends with nobodies; don't be the great somebody.

17-19   Don't hit back; discover beauty in everyone. If you've got it in you, get along with everybody. Don't insist on getting even; that's not for you to do. "I'll do the judging," says God. "I'll take care of it."

20-21   Our Scriptures tell us that if you see your enemy hungry, go buy that person lunch, or if he's thirsty, get him a drink. Your generosity will surprise him with goodness. Don't let evil get the best of you; get the best of evil by doing good.

READ

Read this passage slowly, pausing after each command.

THINK

Laughing and crying with your dearest friends might come easily to you as a woman. However, making friends with nobodies, loving your enemies, and avoiding judgment are a lot more difficult. Our culture preys on the insecurities of women. In a culture that always leaves you wondering if you are thin enough, strong enough, involved enough, smart enough, and so on, exclusion and envy are the norm. But Jesus was not concerned with being a somebody. He gathered in the most unlovely, the most socially awkward, the most unaccomplished in society's eyes, and welcomed them as friends. How will you follow his countercultural footsteps and be a woman of inclusion and forgiveness? A woman who finds beauty in everyone?

PRAY

Write a short request based on each of these commands, engaging specific people in your life. For example, "God, help me to bless _____ even when _____, and to truly share joy with _____." Don't escape into vague application — dive deep into relationships already in place where you can practice these commands.

_____

_____

_____

LIVE

In a world that encourages exclusion and self-exultation, you are called to befriend the "nobodies," love your enemies, and avoid fighting back. Don't be a great "somebody" — we know that in the end that will crumble to nothing. Build on a relational foundation that is of the same enduring material as Jesus — love, self-sacrifice, and humility.

I OBVIOUSLY NEED HELP!

ROMANS 7:17-20,24-25

17-20   But I need something *more*! For if I know the law but still can't keep it, and if the power of sin within me keeps sabotaging my best intentions, I obviously need help! I realize that I don't have what it takes. I can will it, but I can't *do* it. I decide to do good, but I don't *really* do it; I decide not to do bad, but then I do it anyway. My decisions, such as they are, don't result in actions. Something has gone wrong deep within me and gets the better of me every time. . . .

24   I've tried everything and nothing helps. I'm at the end of my rope. Is there no one who can do anything for me? Isn't that the real question?

25   The answer, thank God, is that Jesus Christ can and does. He acted to set things right in this life of contradictions where I want to serve God with all my heart and mind, but am pulled by the influence of sin to do something totally different.

READ

Read the passage through slowly.

THINK

All of us can identify with Paul's sentiments. We have felt helpless as our desire to do good wars with the reality of our actions. What do you think Paul means when he says, "Something has gone wrong deep within me"? Why and how do you think this corruption occurs? How does Jesus' power contrast inability? How does Jesus deal with the root of the problem Paul describes?

PRAY

Thank God for the power of Jesus Christ, which overcomes your deepest, darkest desires and turns your sin nature into a new nature. Ask God for continued perseverance in the battle between what you want to do and what your old self demands. Ask for every fiber of your being to truly be desirous of God's good laws.

LIVE

Paul turns to Jesus as the "cure" for his own internal battles. Today, when you face a struggle between thought and action, consider the Cross and its life-changing power.

AN ORCHARD OF GOOD FRUIT

GALATIANS 5:22-23

22-23 But what happens when we live God's way? He brings gifts into our lives, much the same way that fruit appears in an orchard — things like affection for others, exuberance about life, serenity. We develop a willingness to stick with things, a sense of compassion in the heart, and a conviction that a basic holiness permeates things and people. We find ourselves involved in loyal commitments, not needing to force our way in life, able to marshal and direct our energies wisely.

READ

Read the passage through slowly and allow each portion to sink in.

THINK

This thoughtful rendition of the "fruits of the Spirit" allows room for contemplation. Notice how it is God who is responsible for bringing about these things in our lives — but only when we are living "God's way." Which of these fruits do you see developing in your life as a result of your life with Christ? Which of these do you feel you need the most help "growing"? What are the barriers that make producing this kind of fruit difficult — in your environment, in your heart, and in your vocation?

PRAY

Praise God for bringing gifts into your life — good behaviors and godly habits that surpass what you could do if left to your own devices. Thank God for fruits that he has already developed in you. Pick one quality and pray in detail for God to make it more evident in your life and behaviors. Pray for this same quality to be developed in someone dear to you.

LIVE

Journal about the practical ways you are going to "prepare the soil" for the fruit you desire. Remember that living for God is the root of all good things — faith, not striving.

_____

_____

_____

ENERGETIC IN GOODNESS

TITUS 2:11-14

11-14   God's readiness to give and forgive is now public. Salvation's available for everyone! We're being shown how to turn our backs on a godless, indulgent life, and how to take on a God-filled, God-honoring life. This new life is starting right now, and is whetting our appetites for the glorious day when our great God and Savior, Jesus Christ, appears. He offered himself as a sacrifice to free us from a dark, rebellious life into this good, pure life, making us a people he can be proud of, energetic in goodness.

READ

Imagine the last time you received news so good you could not wait to tell everyone: a promotion, an unexpected visit, a remission of disease. What emotions washed over you? After calling that to mind, read the passage aloud with full enthusiasm.

THINK

Note that Paul is not only thrilled about the prospect of salvation, but also elated about the *process* of salvation, the fact that salvation is already at work in our lives. God is transforming us into "a people he can be proud of." What part of this passage do you find difficult to be excited about, whether from routine or from comprehension? Does salvation and sanctification sometimes seem like a distant thing, in the past and the future? How has God's work already started right now? How have you seen a glimpse of glory in your life already?

PRAY

Ask God for enthusiasm about salvation and the work of salvation. Pray for a sense of *both* long-term hope in what will come when Jesus returns and very present encouragement in the truth of God's work now. Pray for an "energetic goodness" so powerful that it will make people question what they are missing.

LIVE

No matter how low your energy, how great your exhaustion, do not be discouraged. God is making you into a people to be proud of—he is making you into a person of "energetic goodness" no matter what. Journal about how you have already seen God's work of glory in your life and the ways in which you want to become a woman of goodness, purity, and energy in salvation.

_____

_____

_____

GAB OF GRATITUDE

EPHESIANS 5:3-4

3-4   Don't allow love to turn into lust, setting off a downhill slide into sexual promiscuity, filthy practices, or bullying greed. Though some tongues just love the taste of gossip, those who follow Jesus have better uses for language than that. Don't talk dirty or silly. That kind of talk doesn't fit our style. Thanksgiving is our dialect.

READ

Read the passage through, letting each separate piece of wisdom sink in.

THINK

This passage is about the corruption of good gifts — like love and language — into evil things. Consider whether there are some temptations of conversation uniquely difficult for women. What is the purpose of our conversations as Christians? Paul suggests that giving thanks should be our "dialect." An attitude of praise to God can help combat some of the major temptations of twisted language. Consider other forms of "communication" besides face-to-face — how does this passage apply to the way that you use social media, texting, tweeting, e-mailing, and so on?

PRAY

Praise God for the good gift of language — for the ability to communicate with those around you, express emotions, and other benefits of communication often taken for granted. Ask the Spirit for greater awareness — for thought before you speak recklessly or harmfully. Ask instead for good stewardship in the conversations you have and the message you choose to convey.

LIVE

Journal about one space in your life where you feel that you speak with the most Spirit-approval and also one place where you feel most tempted to use your words unwisely. Why? Ponder how you can use thanksgiving as a dialect in both of these places.

HE WENT RIGHT TO WORK

MARK 6:32-34

32-34   So they got in the boat and went off to a remote place by themselves. Someone saw them going and the word got around. From the surrounding towns people went out on foot, running, and got there ahead of them. When Jesus arrived, he saw this huge crowd. At the sight of them, his heart broke — like sheep with no shepherd they were. He went right to work teaching them.

READ

Read the passage slowly, looking for details in setting, tone, and characterization.

THINK

Because Jesus' ministry was related to preaching and healing, he was often going out and going forth. He rarely retreated unless it was necessary, whether for his own restoration or his disciples'. In this passage, he goes to a remote place, yet somehow the word gets out. The people going to him are desperately running and waiting for him to arrive. Put yourself in Jesus' position for a moment. How would you feel if your much-needed getaway was suddenly broken up by strangers who wanted something? By contrast, how does Jesus' response to the people reveal his character? How does it compare to your own? Jesus' response does not mean that you should run yourself ragged when anyone shows up in need — but Jesus' attitude is worth contemplating.

PRAY

Confess your responses to the needy crowds in your life. Be honest about your fears and the ways you have been avoiding them or protecting yourself. Ask God for his compassionate perspective on even the most annoying folks in your community. Confess the less-than-godly ways that you have viewed them — perhaps as nuisances or obligations — and instead ask for eyes to see their lostness and their need.

LIVE

Think about a time when you had an uncompassionate response — inwardly or outwardly. Determine not to repeat the experience today. What are some ways you can develop a heart of compassion for a specific person or group of people who seem to constantly interrupt?

IN BUT NOT OF

JOHN 17:13-19

13-19   Now I'm returning to you. I'm saying these things in the world's hearing so my people can experience my joy completed in them. I gave them your word; the godless world hated them because of it, because they didn't join the world's ways, just as I didn't join the world's ways. I'm not asking that you take them out of the world but that you guard them from the Evil One. They are no more defined by the world than I am defined by the world. Make them holy — consecrated — with the truth; your word is consecrating truth. In the same way that you gave me a mission in the world, I give them a mission in the world. I'm consecrating myself for their sakes so they'll be truth-consecrated in their mission.

READ

Read through this prayer of Jesus for believers slowly and carefully. What words and phrases stand out to you?

THINK

There are multiple facets to Jesus' prayer. Jesus did not pray for you to be removed from the world. If you are no more defined by the world than Jesus was, what do you think that means for your own balance of "in but not of"? Jesus wasn't defined by the world, but he did not confine himself to a remote hilltop either. He was constantly with and caring about people. In what ways does your mission to the world imitate Jesus' balance? Jesus' balance did not come from obeying all of the rules of "holiness" but by obeying the will of the Father to love. Consider your own balance between love and legalism.

PRAY

Thank God for his prayers for you — for his heart of protection and his trust in your freedom. Ask God for the courage to follow Jesus' mission in the world. Pray for wisdom and discernment as you learn what it means to be holy, to be consecrated with the truth and yet not withdrawn from the world you've been sent to.

LIVE

Consider specific actions today to either join in or refrain from. Be sure those choices are motivated by love rather than legalism. Imitate Jesus' example.

HONOR THE MESSAGE

JAMES 4:11-12

11-12 Don't bad-mouth each other, friends. It's God's Word, his Message, his Royal Rule, that takes a beating in that kind of talk. You're supposed to be honoring the Message, not writing graffiti all over it. God is in charge of deciding human destiny. Who do you think you are to meddle in the destiny of others?

READ

Read this passage slowly and carefully, pausing after each poignant phrase.

THINK

Your words are not your own. In the same way that a representative might speak on behalf of a company or a county, your words reflect on the One you serve. The way you speak of others should be more than a casually thrown opinion. What does it mean to "bad-mouth" someone? Don't skirt around the definition so that you come out clean — consider not just the "rule" of gossip but the spirit of it. Consider the kind of conversation that characterizes your meetings with other women and whether or not you are honoring the Message.

PRAY

Repent for making God's message of love look like a message of judgment. Confess conversations where you have assumed too much about those around you or too hastily discarded grace. Pray for the gospel to characterize every word that comes from your lips. Ask for your words to make God look even greater.

LIVE

Write out for yourself your own definition of God's "Royal Rule." How does that translate to your talk about others daily?

_____

_____

_____

GOD WANTS YOU STRONG

EPHESIANS 6:10-12

10-12   And that about wraps it up. God is strong, and he wants you strong. So take everything the Master has set out for you, well-made weapons of the best materials. And put them to use so you will be able to stand up to everything the Devil throws your way. This is no afternoon athletic contest that we'll walk away from and forget about in a couple of hours. This is for keeps, a life-or-death fight to the finish against the Devil and all his angels.

READ

Read the passage slowly and pay attention to the rich imagery.

THINK

In our world, it is so easy to forget about the bigger reality beyond our reality. This spiritual warfare imagery might appeal to men in particular; however, this world is a blazing battle for women. What tailor-made weapons does the Devil throw at you and your sisters in Christ? What lies, fears, and dissensions are aimed particularly at women in this culture? After considering all of this spiritual battle, how do you think Jesus wants you to combat those attacks? What truths can you cling to — what "well-made weapons of the best materials" has he given you?

PRAY

Thank God! Because of Jesus Christ, the battle is already won. Ask for courage and strength in the fights that are still yours to endure, until Jesus returns with the final victory. Confess the wounded places to God — the places where evil already seems to have won a foothold in your life. Ask for strength not only for yourself, but to encourage other women of the faith to battle onward.

LIVE

Consider your best "weapon" for today, whether Scripture, a short, simple prayer, or confidence in a friend. Use it to battle the blows of the Enemy.

ESAU SYNDROME

HEBREWS 12:14-17

14-17   Work at getting along with each other and with God. Otherwise you'll never get so much as a glimpse of God. Make sure no one gets left out of God's generosity. Keep a sharp eye out for weeds of bitter discontent. A thistle or two gone to seed can ruin a whole garden in no time. Watch out for the Esau syndrome: trading away God's lifelong gift in order to satisfy a short-term appetite. You well know how Esau later regretted that impulsive act and wanted God's blessing—but by then it was too late, tears or no tears.

READ

Read the passage through carefully and slowly. Pause and read it through again.

THINK

The idea connecting all of these commands is that how we "get along with" God is very linked to how we get along with one another. God's generosity is the first and only starting point for being generous to others. Without a sense of God's abundant provision and love, the "Esau syndrome" will almost inevitably crop up. What are the short-term temptations that you easily cave to in place of the promised reward? Trusting in God's generosity can help you avoid a ruined garden of the soul — a soul that is met only with disappointment chasing material things.

PRAY

Confess the discontentment growing in your heart. Ask the Spirit to help you identify specific relationships, attitudes, and habits that simply don't demonstrate God's generosity. Ask for glimpses of God's abundant love so that your heart can be opened up to thanksgiving. Ask for mercy to avoid the anxiety from living for short-term pleasures.

LIVE

Avoiding Esau's mistake is as simple as self-control and trust. Today when you are tempted to give in for the "easy" path, think of the long-term goal and the generosity of God.

LEAVING AND RECEIVING

GENESIS 12:1-6

1 GOD told Abram: "Leave your country, your family, and your father's home for a land that I will show you.

2-3
   I'll make you a great nation
      and bless you.
   I'll make you famous;
      you'll be a blessing.
   I'll bless those who bless you;
      those who curse you I'll curse.
   All the families of the Earth
      will be blessed through you."

4-6 So Abram left just as GOD said, and Lot left with him. Abram was seventy-five years old when he left Haran. Abram took his wife Sarai and his nephew Lot with him, along with all the possessions and people they had gotten in Haran, and set out for the land of Canaan and arrived safe and sound.

READ

Read the passage observantly and carefully, looking for details you may not have noticed before. Don't skim.

THINK

When God calls Abram, he tells him to leave everything. For what? For a land that God "will show" him. Notice that God doesn't give the specifics of the neighborhood, good schools in the area, financial-growth plan, cost-risk analysis, or other things that we might take into account before moving. In place of detailed plans, what promise does God make? Instead of asking questions, showing doubt, or second-guessing if God's call will *really* be the most successful, simple endeavor, Abram simply "left just as GOD said." When God asks you to do something for him, do you respond with such faith?

PRAY

Ask God for the faith to follow, without thinking about the potential loss or gain in material goods (or even good reputation). Pray for wisdom and discernment as well—God does not call for recklessness. Also ask for courage in any upcoming decisions in your life, that you and those around you will be able to trust in God's good purposes without knowing all of the details.

LIVE

Journal how you think you might have responded to God's request. Be honest and even humorous if you like. Then, write about how you would like to respond to God's call in the future.

_____

_____

_____

EXCUSES, EXCUSES

EXODUS 4:10-13

10 Moses raised another objection to GOD: "Master, please, I don't talk well. I've never been good with words, neither before nor after you spoke to me. I stutter and stammer."

11-12 GOD said, "And who do you think made the human mouth? And who makes some mute, some deaf, some sighted, some blind? Isn't it I, GOD? So, get going. I'll be right there with you — with your mouth! I'll be right there to teach you what to say."

13 He said, "Oh, Master, please! Send somebody else!"

READ

Read the passage through, trying to imagine the tone on each side of this conversation.

THINK

It may be helpful to remember that this is the third of four objections Moses raises to God's plan. You probably know how this story ends — Moses becomes a mighty leader for one of the greatest acts of salvation described in the Bible. Why do you think this less-than-leader-status moment is included as a part of Moses' story? Do you see some of your own attitudes in Moses? How do you respond to a call, even when God promises his presence and his perfect planning?

PRAY

Confess to God what personal flaw you are using as an excuse. Ask God for renewed confidence and faith in wherever it is he has called you. Thank God for being the Creator of all good things — and also the Creator who uses weaknesses as a part of his purpose. Praise God for not being thwarted by your shortcomings, and ask for a heart that responds with obedience.

LIVE

A willingness to be sent and to trust that your flaws are not big compared to God's power is not just an attitude for huge spiritual undertakings. Today when there is even a small act of service to be done, instead of finding excuses, go forward with a "send me" attitude.

HOLY PLANS FOR YOU

JEREMIAH 1:4-8

4   This is what GOD said:

5   "Before I shaped you in the womb,
          I knew all about you.
       Before you saw the light of day,
          I had holy plans for you:
       A prophet to the nations —
          that's what I had in mind for you."

6   But I said, "Hold it, Master GOD! Look at me.
          I don't know anything. I'm only a boy!"

7-8   GOD told me, "Don't say, 'I'm only a boy.'
          I'll tell you where to go and you'll go there.
       I'll tell you what to say and you'll say it.
          Don't be afraid of a soul.
       I'll be right there, looking after you."
          GOD's Decree.

READ

Read the passage through slowly aloud. Pay attention to the tension and the resolution of the passage.

THINK

What seems to be Jeremiah's main objection to his calling as a prophet? Often, we might assume that with age comes experience, wisdom, influence, and all of the other things that *seem* essential to make an impact. So why is God undeterred by Jeremiah's youth? God is ultimately in charge of Jeremiah's mission — his words, his destination, and his reception. Although you might not be called to be a prophet, are there other callings and tasks in your life that you feel ill-equipped for? What does this passage reveal about the way God works through you and what it is God "needs" from his chosen people?

PRAY

Come clean to God about your insecurities, whether a lack of experience or some other fundamental flaw. Be open with him about your uncertainty. Ask God for confidence in his calling — not a confidence in your own abilities, but in his holy purposes, planned out before you could even know them. Praise him for working through the "least of these," which includes you.

LIVE

Don't be afraid of what you lack. Trust that God is with you and that he will not allow his purposes to fail, no matter how small your résumé seems.

THE BLAME GAME

EXODUS 32:19-24

19-20 When Moses came near to the camp and saw the calf and the people dancing, his anger flared. He threw down the tablets and smashed them to pieces at the foot of the mountain. He took the calf that they had made, melted it down with fire, pulverized it to powder, then scattered it on the water and made the Israelites drink it.

21 Moses said to Aaron, "What on Earth did these people ever do to you that you involved them in this huge sin?"

22-23 Aaron said, "Master, don't be angry. You know this people and how set on evil they are. They said to me, 'Make us gods who will lead us. This Moses, the man who brought us out of Egypt, we don't know what's happened to him.'

24 "So I said, 'Who has gold?' And they took off their jewelry and gave it to me. I threw it in the fire and out came this calf."

READ

Read the passage through carefully and observantly, paying special attention to the tone of the speakers. Don't miss the humor.

THINK

Moses has entrusted the leadership of the Israelites to Aaron. Although he punishes the Israelites as a whole, he holds Aaron specifically accountable. What are Aaron's tactics when confronted with his failure as a leader? Do any of those verbal moves look familiar to you? How do you respond when confronted about your sin by God or by others in your community?

PRAY

Be honest with God about the golden calves you've made. Admit truly and completely your role in the sin in your life and the way in which you have encouraged others to sin, consciously or unconsciously. Ask God for forgiveness and for the best way to take ownership of your sins. Ask especially for grace and transparency in the places where you are a leader. Ask the Spirit to guide you into taking more responsibility, not less, and to guide you toward true repentance.

LIVE

Go through the day without casting any blame on others, spoken or unspoken. Instead focus on righteous living and fruitful work.

SURGE OF HOSPITALITY

ACTS 16:13-15

13-14 On the Sabbath, we left the city and went down along the river where we had heard there was to be a prayer meeting. We took our place with the women who had gathered there and talked with them. One woman, Lydia, was from Thyatira and a dealer in expensive textiles, known to be a God-fearing woman. As she listened with intensity to what was being said, the Master gave her a trusting heart — and she believed!

15 After she was baptized, along with everyone in her household, she said in a surge of hospitality, "If you're confident that I'm in this with you and believe in the Master truly, come home with me and be my guests." We hesitated, but she wouldn't take no for an answer.

READ

Imagine this encounter between the disciples and the woman Lydia. What sights and sounds can you picture in the setting? What emotions do you think the characters went through?

THINK

Lydia is clearly a leader in the household—a successful woman who listens "with intensity" to the gospel of Jesus. She seems to be the one who was responsible for leading her entire household to faith, setting an example in her trust and faith. The story doesn't stop there, however. Luke seems to find it important to also write about her invitation to the disciples. There seems to be a pattern—the Master "gave her a trusting heart" and in response, Lydia was also moved to giving. Generosity is the sign and seal of salvation—an outpouring of grace just as we experience it in Christ. What is your response to the trusting heart God has given you?

PRAY

Ask God for a greater understanding of his gifts, and that that in turn will lead you to be giving and generous toward others. Pray for specific ways to show hospitality to those around you. Pray for a spirit of openhandedness, for a "surge of hospitality" to characterize your interactions with others.

LIVE

Journal about simple ways you can imitate a "surge of hospitality" in your own life. It does not necessarily have to mean having people into your own home.

_____

_____

_____

GIVING EXTRAVAGANTLY

LUKE 21:1-4

1-4 Just then he looked up and saw the rich people dropping offerings in the collection plate. Then he saw a poor widow put in two pennies. He said, "The plain truth is that this widow has given by far the largest offering today. All these others made offerings that they'll never miss; she gave extravagantly what she couldn't afford — she gave her all!"

READ

Read this familiar passage slowly and observantly. Don't assume you have it down. Receive it again for the first time.

THINK

Widows in the time of Jesus were on the fringes of society. Apart from their husbands or their households, they had no income, no real status, and sometimes no real hope of remarriage. The rich people are not being scorned or berated by Jesus — they are in fact doing their duty. Yet, Jesus particularly praises the widow. Why? This is not just a lesson about finances — the attitude exhibited is much bigger than money alone. Where are you feeling tight and pressed? Is it time, emotional energy, patience with others, or something else? How does giving free you from anxiety?

PRAY

Ask God for the courage to give freely and extravagantly, beyond what you feel you can afford. Thank him for his provision, which will keep going even when it seems impossible. Praise him for his abundant blessings, and ask for the ability to imitate his generosity.

LIVE

Generosity lives in actions, not just ideas. Whatever it is you think you don't have enough of, give it and trust that God will provide.

WIND AND SEA AT HIS BECK AND CALL

MARK 4:35-41

35-38   Late that day he said to them, "Let's go across to the other side." They took him in the boat as he was. Other boats came along. A huge storm came up. Waves poured into the boat, threatening to sink it. And Jesus was in the stern, head on a pillow, sleeping! They roused him, saying, "Teacher, is it nothing to you that we're going down?"

39-40   Awake now, he told the wind to pipe down and said to the sea, "Quiet! Settle down!" The wind ran out of breath; the sea became smooth as glass. Jesus reprimanded the disciples: "Why are you such cowards? Don't you have any faith at all?"

41   They were in absolute awe, staggered. "Who is this, anyway?" they asked. "Wind and sea at his beck and call!"

READ

Read the passage slowly and attentively. Try to imagine the sights, sounds, and emotions of the scene.

THINK

What is the main impression of Jesus given by this description? This goes beyond keeping your cool in a crisis. This is about absolute power. When the disciples woke up Jesus, do you think they were expecting this response or were they simply wanting him to bail out some water with buckets like they were? Jesus is not just a teacher, some life coach, or a dispenser of proverbs — he is absolute Lord of all creation, the Master who is never caught off guard or alarmed by bad circumstances. What does that show you about Jesus' role in your own life? What emotions do you most resonate with in this story? The fear? The awe? The calm certainty?

PRAY

Praise God, the Creator and Sustainer of life, who is never frightened by a storm. Thank God, the all-powerful and all-knowing, for being the One who orchestrates all things. Ask God for the strength to trust in his absolute goodness, even when events seem chaotic or hopeless. Cling to the identity of Jesus as Lord of all and as *your* Lord and Savior.

LIVE

Write about a storm you found yourself in recently and the ways in which Jesus calmed it and brought you through.

_____

_____

_____

SELF-SACRIFICE, NOT SELF-HELP

MARK 8:34-37

34-37　Calling the crowd to join his disciples, he said, "Anyone who intends to come with me has to let me lead. You're not in the driver's seat; *I* am. Don't run from suffering; embrace it. Follow me and I'll show you how. Self-help is no help at all. Self-sacrifice is the way, my way, to saving yourself, your true self. What good would it do to get everything you want and lose you, the real you? What could you ever trade your soul for?"

READ

Read the passage carefully and observantly.

THINK

Consider the difference between self-help and self-sacrifice. Self-sacrifice isn't about completely ignoring self-esteem, thinking you're a worm. Instead it's about redefining where worth comes from and living accordingly. Does our culture respond well to the idea of self-sacrifice or does it promote pampering? Suffering often seems like an idea relevant to persecuted Christians in other countries — but Jesus is asking us to embrace it to receive your "true self." What does suffering reveal about us versus God? What's the distinction between the kind of self-discovery promised by self-help and the truth promised by Jesus through the Cross?

PRAY

Ask God for the courage to "lose yourself" in order to truly find yourself in him. Pray against the lies of culture that tell us to protect ourselves and keep ourselves safe from the risky investment of love and eternal life. Thank God for his grace and mercy, which surpasses anything you could possibly "save" by being cautious on this earth. Ask for your life choices to be guided by self-sacrifice, not self-help.

LIVE

When the world says, "Take care of yourself," with your actions say, "Christ first" and "Others first." Throw yourself into the freedom of the Cross.

WOMAN WHO STICKS WITH GOD

JEREMIAH 17:7-10

7-8
Blessed is the man who trusts me, GOD,
    the woman who sticks with GOD.
They're like trees replanted in Eden,
    putting down roots near the rivers —
Never a worry through the hottest of summers,
    never dropping a leaf,
Serene and calm through droughts,
    bearing fresh fruit every season.

9-10
The heart is hopelessly dark and deceitful,
    a puzzle that no one can figure out.
But I, GOD, search the heart
    and examine the mind.
I get to the heart of the human.
    I get to the root of things.
I treat them as they really are,
    not as they pretend to be.

READ

Read the passage through slowly. Visualize all of the rich images presented in the text. Pause to reflect.

THINK

Think about the calming cool of tree shade in the hot summer or the brightness of fruit splashed against green leaves. This is the metaphor given for those who trust God. Does that serenity, that freshness, seem like a part of your life or does it seem like a distant dream? The writer references not just any garden, but specifically Eden. Trust in the Lord doesn't just provide tranquility — it restores a hint of Paradise. By contrast, the human heart is usually a tangled mess. Where do you see the "puzzles" in your own heart and in the hearts of those around you? God ultimately understands — and forgives — the tangled parts of your heart and provides calm. What is required of you to receive that gift?

PRAY

Confess to God the puzzles of your heart. Dig deep and ask the Spirit to uncover the deceptions, twists, and turns that only God could understand. Ask for forgiveness. Ask God for the sort of trust that leads to fruitfulness and calm tranquility — cry out for a deep rootedness in him that cannot be shaken.

LIVE

Let your actions be guided by *trust* in God, not the impulses and urges of your heart. Walk forward into what you know cannot fail.

IT'S QUITE SIMPLE

MICAH 6:6-8

6-7 How can I stand up before GOD
          and show proper respect to the high God?
      Should I bring an armload of offerings
          topped off with yearling calves?
      Would GOD be impressed with thousands of rams,
          with buckets and barrels of olive oil?
      Would he be moved if I sacrificed my firstborn child,
          my precious baby, to cancel my sin?

8 But he's already made it plain how to live, what to do,
          what GOD is looking for in men and women.
      It's quite simple: Do what is fair and just to your neighbor,
          be compassionate and loyal in your love,
      And don't take yourself too seriously —
          take God seriously.

READ

Read the passage as question and answer, a sort of catechism just for you.

THINK

The quintessential question behind the first part of the text is, What could God, the Almighty, really be impressed with? Don't get distracted by the goats and rams — you too might be tempted to offer up legalistic "sacrifices." Is he really impressed with your church attendance, or the length of your devotionals? Of course the answer is provided almost as soon as you ask the question — it points out the silliness of thinking "stuff" can impress God, doesn't it? Instead God wants something much simpler. How would you describe or sum up the "commandments" God gives? How can they be applied in your own life?

PRAY

Praise God for his absolute power. He doesn't need to be pacified with presents. Thank him for a love so big it's beyond purchasing. In prayer, take time to ask for each of these parts of true, godly, simple living and their specific applications in your life and work.

LIVE

Don't take yourself too seriously. You and your sacrifices aren't that big. But God is — and he loves you. He only asks for your trust and simple love today.

GOD WILL NEVER LET YOU DOWN

1 CORINTHIANS 10:12-13

12   Don't be so naive and self-confident. You're not exempt. You could fall flat on your face as easily as anyone else. Forget about self-confidence; it's useless. Cultivate God-confidence.

13   No test or temptation that comes your way is beyond the course of what others have had to face. All you need to remember is that God will never let you down; he'll never let you be pushed past your limit; he'll always be there to help you come through it.

READ

Read the passage, slowly and carefully, several times through.

THINK

Do the tests and temptations in front of you feel completely overwhelming? Shameful? Have you ever felt like you are the only one who is struggling with something, or the only one engaged in a monumental task? The idea that you are alone is exactly what the Enemy wants. It inflates your pride by skewing your sense of justice — or it increases your shame, making you unwilling to seek help. There is no new and special sin or unique struggle — at the core, evil is simply evil from generation to generation. But, God does not allow you to be put into a place where it is impossible to receive help. Has he helped you in the past? How much more will he help you now?

PRAY

Praise God for the trials and tests, great and small, that he has led you through in the past and saved you from. Thank him for his unfailing rescue. Be honest with God about the temptations that feel beyond you, that seem past what you are capable of handling. Ask for the path of escape toward him and righteousness.

LIVE

When we are tempted, the first thing to become skewed is our understanding of God and our understanding of ourselves. Journal about God-confidence — trust in the One who is faithful to deliver you.

_____

_____

_____

THE HIGH PRIVILEGE OF KNOWING CHRIST JESUS

PHILIPPIANS 3:7-11

7-9   The very credentials these people are waving around as something special, I'm tearing up and throwing out with the trash—along with everything else I used to take credit for. And why? Because of Christ. Yes, all the things I once thought were so important are gone from my life. Compared to the high privilege of knowing Christ Jesus as my Master, firsthand, everything I once thought I had going for me is insignificant—dog dung. I've dumped it all in the trash so that I could embrace Christ and be embraced by him. I didn't want some petty, inferior brand of righteousness that comes from keeping a list of rules when I could get the robust kind that comes from trusting Christ—*God's* righteousness.

10-11 I gave up all that inferior stuff so I could know Christ personally, experience his resurrection power, be a partner in his suffering, and go all the way with him to death itself. If there was any way to get in on the resurrection from the dead, I wanted to do it.

READ

Read the passage slowly and deeply. Notice sharp and surprising images, deep phrases and big ideas.

THINK

Comparing the things around us to "dog dung" might seem a little alarming in a devotional, but it is not at all far from Paul's original word. How important are credentials and qualifications in your world? How much time have you spent concerning yourself with whether you are certified enough, trained enough, educated enough, experienced enough for the tasks you find yourself in, from accounting to motherhood? Compared to knowing Jesus, all of those things, according to Paul, can be tossed away with trophies and treasures — and if they stop you from knowing Jesus, perhaps they should be. Accomplishments are not bad. But are they worth more to you than the pursuit of Jesus? Would you be willing to trade your status for an intimate knowledge of Jesus' love, even if no one ever saw it?

PRAY

Consider all of the things that set you apart and make you special by the world's standards — and perhaps by your own, too. Praise God for giving you those good things, and spend time surrendering them back into his hands. Ask for a thirst to know Jesus, no matter what the cost.

LIVE

Put things in perspective today. When it's standing beside the cross, is it worth anxiety? Leave whatever hinders you from Jesus at the foot of the cross without concern of what others might think.

MISSING JESUS

JOHN 5:39-44

39-40 You have your heads in your Bibles constantly because you think you'll find eternal life there. But you miss the forest for the trees. These Scriptures are all about *me*! And here I am, standing right before you, and you aren't willing to receive from me the life you say you want.

41-44 I'm not interested in crowd approval. And do you know why? Because I know you and your crowds. I know that love, especially God's love, is not on your working agenda. I came with the authority of my Father, and you either dismiss me or avoid me. If another came, acting self-important, you would welcome him with open arms. How do you expect to get anywhere with God when you spend all your time jockeying for position with each other, ranking your rivals and ignoring God?

READ

Read the passage carefully, paying attention to the overall tone as well as specific phrases that stand out to you.

THINK

Jesus is speaking here to the religious folk of his day. The equivalent of "good Christian people" back then were outraged by what seemed to be Jesus' bad theology: his claim that God was his Father and that he had the power of God himself. Do you ever find yourself so overwhelmed with church stuff that you can't really *see* Jesus? Since a relationship with Christ is the origin and end goal of all righteous activities, any "good" thing you are doing loses its meaning without the person of Christ. Often your "working agenda" might contradict God's plan of love — which is sometimes spontaneous, often messy, and always sacrificial. It is easy to distance ourselves from those who physically rejected and wounded the historical person of Jesus — but are there ways in which you dismiss and avoid Jesus in the midst of your own religious behavior?

PRAY

Ask the Spirit to reveal any mixed-up motives in your churchly and "good" activities. Pray earnestly that you would have the eyes to see all of the radical love and life-changing grace of *Jesus* instead of focusing on the details that make you feel important or safe. Ask God to release you from the temptation to better your Christian standing with delusions of grandeur. Seek true humility by contemplating the way Jesus came — not as a self-important king. Jesus came claiming the authority and love of the Father that overrode any human agenda. Praise him for redefining spiritual health, and ask him to help you understand and apply it.

LIVE

102

Whatever is on your "working agenda," let God's love, as shown by Jesus Christ, be more important. Look for Jesus and seek to walk in his footsteps.

FAITH-LIFE SHOWS ITS COLORS

JAMES 1:2-4

2-4 Consider it a sheer gift, friends, when tests and challenges come at you from all sides. You know that under pressure, your faith-life is forced into the open and shows its true colors. So don't try to get out of anything prematurely. Let it do its work so you become mature and well-developed, not deficient in any way.

READ

Read the passage slowly and thoroughly.

THINK

You can usually tell what is deep inside of a person based on how they respond to tough situations. It is easy to mask our fears and anxieties in the day-to-day — but loss, uncertainty, and pain make it almost impossible to keep up the act. Have you ever known anyone robbed of challenge or who chose never to be uncomfortable? What result does that have? Consider that God's purpose in allowing you to go through trials is not to cause pain, but to bring growth. In what ways are pressures, difficulties, tests, and challenges essential to maturity? A good parent does not just protect — a good parent equips. Consider how God mirrors that tough part of parenthood to you.

PRAY

Consider the challenges and tests that are in your life right now. Whether it's a task, a relationship, or an emotional hurdle, confess to God if you've been trying to escape it or are afraid of the difficulty. Ask the Spirit to truly reveal the gift of challenge in your life. Pray for growth, not just escape. Plead for rescue that will develop your spiritual bones and muscles.

LIVE

Look at each new challenge and test as another opportunity to receive something, not simply survive.

UNINTIMIDATED AND BEAUTIFUL

1 PETER 3:3-6

3-4 What matters is not your outer appearance — the styling of your hair, the jewelry you wear, the cut of your clothes — but your inner disposition.

4-6 Cultivate inner beauty, the gentle, gracious kind that God delights in. The holy women of old were beautiful before God that way, and were good, loyal wives to their husbands. Sarah, for instance, taking care of Abraham, would address him as "my dear husband." You'll be true daughters of Sarah if you do the same, unanxious and unintimidated.

READ

Read this passage slowly, looking for words and phrases that seem new to you. Observe. Receive.

THINK

At the root of our culture's obsession with looks is a fundamental lack of trust. Even if we feel worthless inside, enough pricey fixes and flattering cuts might trick us into the sense that we have more value—to men, to the world at large, and to ourselves. Peter holds up "inner beauty," but not as some kind of Amish avoidance of the glamorous. Instead, he uses the words "unanxious" and "unintimidated" in the same passage that he discusses "gentle" and "gracious" beauty. He holds up Sarah's care and respect of Abraham as an example of a loving, submissive relationship and simultaneously of courage. Is inner beauty, the kind that God values, inherent or is it something that we work toward? What is the poisonous belief about outer appearance that you find hard to combat? How do you see God bestowing inner beauty on you through Jesus?

PRAY

Confess to God the things about outer appearance that ensnare you. It may not be something so obvious as too much time preening—most likely you will have to ask the Spirit to help you dig deeper and reveal the insecurities deep down. Thank God for the inner beauty that he values above all, and praise him for the ways in which he has already given you loveliness-of-soul—in your faith, in your relationships, and in your own character, which he formed and fashioned. Ask for help combatting appearance anxiety and for discernment to develop a lovely, beautiful character.

LIVE

Write about the inner beauty that you want to develop further as you walk with Jesus. Pick a specific character trait, habit, or relationship you want to develop into something lovely. How will you fight anxiety?

REAL WISDOM

JAMES 3:13-18

13-16   Do you want to be counted wise, to build a reputation for wisdom? Here's what you do: Live well, live wisely, live humbly. It's the way you live, not the way you talk, that counts. Mean-spirited ambition isn't wisdom. Boasting that you are wise isn't wisdom. Twisting the truth to make yourselves sound wise isn't wisdom. It's the furthest thing from wisdom — it's animal cunning, devilish conniving. Whenever you're trying to look better than others or get the better of others, things fall apart and everyone ends up at the others' throats.

17-18   Real wisdom, God's wisdom, begins with a holy life and is characterized by getting along with others. It is gentle and reasonable, overflowing with mercy and blessings, not hot one day and cold the next, not two-faced. You can develop a healthy, robust community that lives right with God and enjoy its results *only* if you do the hard work of getting along with each other, treating each other with dignity and honor.

READ

Read the passage slowly and carefully, pausing after phrases that resonate with you. Read the passage again.

THINK

In our world, "wisdom" can be defined as anything from a calm veneer to successful know-how. However, this passage points out the danger of trying to appear wise. It can make us self-important and dismissive of others. How have you seen the difference between striving to look better than others and striving to live better for Jesus in your life? Have you been in a situation where competition has led to everyone being at one another's throats? What is the antidote to that sort of poisonous community and how does Jesus want you to help bring it about? True wisdom begins and ends in love.

PRAY

Confess to God your mistreatment of others in order to look good. Repent for merely talking wisely instead of living wisely. Ask God for the true wisdom that comes from him, especially as it relates to living with others. Invite God to teach you humility and to guide you into relationships — personal and professional — free of manipulation. Ask for the courage to seek wisdom from its source instead of looking for the end result of praise.

LIVE

Wisely — and prayerfully relying on God — treat those around you with "dignity and honor" today, even if they seem dishonorable.

LEARN A LIFE OF LOVE

EPHESIANS 5:1-2

1-2 Watch what God does, and then you do it, like children who learn proper behavior from their parents. Mostly what God does is love you. Keep company with him and learn a life of love. Observe how Christ loved us. His love was not cautious but extravagant. He didn't love in order to get something from us but to give everything of himself to us. Love like that.

READ

Read this short passage slowly and carefully.

THINK

It is amazing how much children pick up on. Often, adults might not even be aware of the tone or phrases they use without hearing them parroted back. Children watch closely — and their imitation comes from a longing to be accepted and embraced by the people they look up to, the grown-ups. If you are to imitate God like a child takes after their parent, how can you best "keep company" with God and so "learn a life of love"? What point does Paul make about motivation and not just the external actions of love, but the internal purpose behind what we do?

PRAY

Thank God for his parental care and for his wise and wonderful lessons. Ask for greater understanding of his extravagant and incautious love, and invite him to teach you what a "life of love" looks like.

LIVE

Carry the love of Christ in your heart and mind so that in each encounter you have, you will be inclined to imitate him. Love without an agenda.

THE HIGHEST RANK IN GOD'S KINGDOM

MATTHEW 18:1-5

1   At about the same time, the disciples came to Jesus asking, "Who gets the highest rank in God's kingdom?"

2-5   For an answer Jesus called over a child, whom he stood in the middle of the room, and said, "I'm telling you, once and for all, that unless you return to square one and start over like children, you're not even going to get a look at the kingdom, let alone get in. Whoever becomes simple and elemental again, like this child, will rank high in God's kingdom. What's more, when you receive the childlike on my account, it's the same as receiving me."

READ

Read the passage, imagining the scene and where you might be standing, what emotions you might feel, and what questions you might have.

THINK

"Faith like a child" is a common phrase in sermons and devotionals, but what sort of an attitude do you think it describes? What prevents you from being "childlike" before the Lord? Note the attitude of the disciples' question, and observe that Jesus doesn't exactly "answer" their question. Have you ever found yourself scrambling for prestige and impatient for order? See how Jesus addresses that attitude even while avoiding an exact answer. What is it about the kingdom of God that demands not rank but childlikeness?

PRAY

Confess to God the "grown-up" stuff that gets in between you and him. Ask the Spirit to help you examine the "rank" you're concerned with, in the kingdom and in your daily life. Ask Jesus to reveal the childlike spirit he wants you to have. Praise him for requiring something so marvelously simple from his followers. Ask for a vision of the kingdom.

LIVE

Simplicity in our culture has to be chosen, not simply hoped for. What will you do to make your approach to God more like a child's?

MIGHTY WARRIOR

JUDGES 6:11-14

11-12 One day the angel of GOD came and sat down under the oak in Ophrah that belonged to Joash the Abiezrite, whose son Gideon was threshing wheat in the winepress, out of sight of the Midianites. The angel of GOD appeared to him and said, "GOD is with you, O mighty warrior!"

13 Gideon replied, "With *me*, my master? If GOD is with us, why has all this happened to us? Where are all the miracle-wonders our parents and grandparents told us about, telling us, 'Didn't GOD deliver us from Egypt?' The fact is, GOD has nothing to do with us—he has turned us over to Midian."

14 But GOD faced him directly: "Go in this strength that is yours. Save Israel from Midian. Haven't I just sent you?"

READ

Read the passage slowly, observing all of the subtleties of the narrative.

THINK

When the angel of God finds Gideon, he is "out of sight of the Midianites." The text doesn't say that he is *hiding* exactly, but you can assume that Gideon is definitely not a soldier by trade based on where the reader first "sees" him. Yet, the angel refers to him as "mighty warrior" before he has a sword in hand or a thought beyond self-preservation. Do you resonate with Gideon's response? Do you ever feel like if God was truly with you and your community, there would be more miracles and less fear? Instead of responding to the complaint, God tells Gideon that he is the one with the strength to save Israel, sent by God for the purpose of delivery. Do you ever complain about your surroundings, trying to avoid conflict, when perhaps you are called to something more "mighty"?

PRAY

If you feel as though God doesn't really seem present, confess that honestly to him in prayer. Ask God to give you a new perspective on the events around you. If he seems distant from your circumstances, perhaps it is because you need to walk forward in faith and action. If you feel ill-equipped, the opposite of a mighty warrior for God, ask to be filled with a sense of true identity, strength, and purpose in Christ. You are more than a conqueror.

LIVE

You may not be who you think you are. You might in fact be a mighty warrior for the Lord, called not to complain but to complete a mighty task by relying on his strength. Don't hide from the sight of conflict—walk forward in faith.

SACRIFICE AND WORSHIP

1 SAMUEL 1:23-26

23-24   Elkanah said to his wife, "Do what you think is best. Stay home until you have weaned him. Yes! Let GOD complete what he has begun!"

So she did. She stayed home and nursed her son until she had weaned him. Then she took him up to Shiloh, bringing also the makings of a generous sacrificial meal — a prize bull, flour, and wine. The child was so young to be sent off!

25-26   They first butchered the bull, then brought the child to Eli. Hannah said, "Excuse me, sir. Would you believe that I'm the very woman who was standing before you at this very spot, praying to GOD? I prayed for this child, and GOD gave me what I asked for. And now I have dedicated him to GOD. He's dedicated to GOD for life."

Then and there, they worshiped GOD.

READ

Whatever you know of Hannah's story, read the passage slowly and carefully, trying to imagine the emotions of the scene afresh. Put yourself in her position as you read along.

THINK

Hannah's story is one of sorrow and longing for much of her life. She prays faithfully for a child, facing the scorn of those who judge her as a failure for being unable to conceive. When God grants her request, instead of clinging to what she always prayed for, she faithfully returns it. Are you a mother or do you know a mother? Can you imagine the bonding of breast-feeding followed by giving up a beloved child? Not only does Hannah part with her dearest treasure, she gives an expensive praise offering to God to send with their son to the temple. At the end of the passage, Hannah and her husband are not depicted grimly doing their duty, but instead they "worshiped God." Can you imagine this sort of trust and generosity with something that God has given you? Are you inclined to give back what he gives?

PRAY

Contemplate the deep longings of your heart. Whether it's a specific event or a hoped-for relationship, what sort of things do you ache for? Like Hannah did, ask God to grant those desires. If he already has granted you those things in the past, praise him and thank him and ask for the courage to "give it back" — whether that means trusting him with a child or simply giving something away. Worship God, who gives all good gifts, and ask for a heart of gratitude.

LIVE

Write about how you will "give back" what God has given to you today. It may not be a simple action but instead an attitude of the heart. Demonstrate trust.

_____

_____

_____

MONEY DECEIVES

HABAKKUK 2:4-6

4 Look at that man, bloated by self-importance —
  full of himself but soul-empty.
But the person in right standing before God
  through loyal and steady believing
  is fully alive, *really* alive.

5-6 Note well: Money deceives.
  The arrogant rich don't last.
They are more hungry for wealth
  than the grave is for cadavers.
Like death, they always want more,
  but the "more" they get is dead bodies.
They are cemeteries filled with dead nations,
  graveyards filled with corpses.
Don't give people like this a second thought.
  Soon the whole world will be taunting them.

READ

Read the passage slowly and carefully. Pause and read through it again, aloud.

THINK

It is possible to be "bloated by self-importance" — so stuffed with stuff — yet empty inside. This passage specifically warns against the damages of seeking wealth, but is there another type of "more" that is addicting and deceiving in your life? What does it mean to be "soul-empty"? Do you ever feel that way or do you know people who seem that way? In what ways are you tempted to be self-important but not truly full with the Spirit and contentment in God?

PRAY

Confess to God the bloating self-importance that has you trying to find satisfaction apart from him. Ask for help searching your heart for the "more" that you desire — whether it's status, time, control, or something else. Ask God to free you from bondage to that destructive behavior. Praise the God of resurrection who can lift you out of any materialistic grave. Ask to be made "fully alive" in him.

LIVE

Journal about the deception of "more" in your life and seek true life in Jesus today instead.

_____

_____

_____

LEAKING CISTERNS

JEREMIAH 2:12-13

12-13   "Stand in shock, heavens, at what you see!
                Throw up your hands in disbelief—this can't be!"
                        God's Decree.
        "My people have committed a compound sin:
                they've walked out on me, the fountain
        Of fresh flowing waters, and then dug cisterns—
                cisterns that leak, cisterns that are no better than sieves."

READ

Read the passage slowly and carefully, focusing on the imagery.

THINK

Who would drink from a dirty, sun-hot, metallic water fountain when they could have fresh, cold, purified water? While the context here is Israel turning away from God to worship idols, the imagery still applies to all of us who claim to follow Jesus and yet struggle with sin. Sin is, first of all, turning away from God's good, pure, beautiful gifts — rejection. Do you see situations in your life where you reject God's gifts or take them too lightly? Sin is then not only rejecting God, but replacing him with something inferior and doomed to fail. What broken cisterns do you try to use to satisfy your deep, spiritual thirst? Is it broken relationships, overworking, distracting yourself silly with entertainment? Or something else?

PRAY

Ask God to reveal the broken cisterns in your life. Confess the places you have been going to satisfy your thirst that simply won't cut it. Praise God for his good gifts — for the free-flowing, beautiful "water" he provides to satisfy your deepest needs. Ask for mercy and conviction in turning to him, instead of away from him. Ask for your "tastes" to incline toward his good gifts.

LIVE

When you find yourself going toward your familiar but unsatisfying broken cistern, be aware of your actions. If possible, physically walk away. Pursue the satisfaction God gives. Shift gears.

SUNRISE FROM SUNSET

PSALM 103:6-18

6-18   GOD makes everything come out right;
            he puts victims back on their feet.
        He showed Moses how he went about his work,
            opened up his plans to all Israel.
        God is sheer mercy and grace;
            not easily angered, he's rich in love.
        He doesn't endlessly nag and scold,
            nor hold grudges forever.
        He doesn't treat us as our sins deserve,
            nor pay us back in full for our wrongs.
        As high as heaven is over the earth,
            so strong is his love to those who fear him.
        And as far as sunrise is from sunset,
            he has separated us from our sins.
        As parents feel for their children,
            GOD feels for those who fear him.
        He knows us inside and out,
            keeps in mind that we're made of mud.

READ

Read the passage slowly, savoring all of the words in the passage.

THINK

Just like a parent, God knows that we're small and dependent because we're his creation — "we're made of mud." Unlike earthly parents, however, God's love is perfect. He is able not only to "put up with" shortcomings, but to remove them completely, as far as the east is from the west. Do you see God as this type of a Father? Do you ever feel afraid that God is easily angered? Do you live in anxiety that God is a scolding Father or a merciless judge? How does this passage speak to God's love and your place inside of it?

PRAY

Confess to God any warped images you might have of who he is. Ask the Spirit to reveal to you the dark corners in your heart where you treat God too much like an earthly parent or a distant judge. Praise him for his power, for his plan to make all things right and set you back on your feet. Thank him for his endless, purifying love that is not content to simply hold you, but works to change and redeem you.

LIVE

Live secure in the knowledge that God's love doesn't give up on you and always works toward your greatest good, every single day.

GOOD WORK FOR A GOOD MASTER

COLOSSIANS 3:22-25

22-25 Servants, do what you're told by your earthly masters. And don't just do the minimum that will get you by. Do your best. Work from the heart for your real Master, for God, confident that you'll get paid in full when you come into your inheritance. Keep in mind always that the ultimate Master you're serving is Christ. The sullen servant who does shoddy work will be held responsible. Being a follow of Jesus doesn't cover up bad work.

READ

Read through the passage slowly and carefully. Imagine that Paul is speaking to twenty-first-century Christians.

THINK

In this fallen world, the chances are high that you are overworked, underpaid, or underappreciated—perhaps all of the above. Although work was originally made to be good (the Garden of Eden wasn't a vacation), after the Fall it has become toil—and in some cases that is more obvious than others. Paul is encouraging believers to do their best even in these fallen circumstances, because the true Master of all endeavors is Jesus. It's important to note that Paul doesn't say, "Work until you drop" or "Do your best so that you climb the ladder." Instead he says "work from the heart" for the true inheritance of Jesus' joy, from which no taxes are taken, from which no anxiety stems. What does it mean in your daily work to do your best and work from the heart?

PRAY

Ask the Spirit of God for wisdom and discernment in how to do your best. Repent of any grumbling related to work, whether compensation, coworkers, or authority. Ask the Spirit for a heart of integrity in your daily practices. Remember that God is the giver of all good gifts, and nothing is purposeless. Invite God to give you a full heart for good work, even if no one else will reward you.

LIVE

Journal about your frustrations with work. Then, write about how you can work more fully from your heart, for God and not for men.

GETTING GOD-REALITY

LUKE 12:29-32

29-32   What I'm trying to do here is get you to relax, not be so preoccupied with *getting* so you can respond to God's *giving*. People who don't know God and the way he works fuss over these things, but you know both God and how he works. Steep yourself in God-reality, God-initiative, God-provisions. You'll find all your everyday human concerns will be met. Don't be afraid of missing out. You're my dearest friends! The Father wants to give you the very kingdom itself.

READ

Read these words of Jesus slowly and carefully, allowing all of it to sink in.

THINK

Are you preoccupied with *getting*? Is it "enough" financial support, "a little more" in shape, "finding" more time, or some other "getting" that occupies your daily thoughts and deeds? The passage tells us that being distracted with *getting* can take our focus away from God's *giving*. Knowing God should change how you view even what seems the most "necessary." He is Provider, Creator, Sustainer. He is the giver of all good things, and he is the one in charge of the cosmos. A 2 percent raise or five pounds lost is nothing compared to the power of raising Jesus from the dead and freely giving eternal life. Why is Jesus warning his disciples about this? How does Jesus remind his disciples about *their* identity to further "prove" his point?

PRAY

Confess to God the "getting" that is causing you to ignore the "giving." Ask for help releasing any anxiety and stress you feel. Praise God for all of the ways he has already provided for you. Thank him for inviting you into the kingdom, and ask for a heart that yearns for God's freedom and God's actions instead of frantically trying to work toward your own. Pray for ways to steep yourself in the reality of the kingdom instead of what seems so essential and urgent on earth.

LIVE

How has "getting" gotten in the way of God's "giving" in the past? How has it affected *your* giving to others? Journal about how gratitude can surpass anxiety.

GOD'S LAVISH ATTENTION

DEUTERONOMY 32:10-14

10-14   He found him out in the wilderness,
          in an empty, windswept wasteland.
    He threw his arms around him, lavished attention on him,
          guarding him as the apple of his eye.
    He was like an eagle hovering over its nest,
          overshadowing its young,
    Then spreading its wings, lifting them into the air,
          teaching them to fly.
    GOD alone led him;
          there was not a foreign god in sight.
    GOD lifted him onto the hilltops,
          so he could feast on the crops in the fields.
    He fed him honey from the rock,
          oil from granite crags,
    Curds of cattle and the milk of sheep,
          the choice cuts of lambs and goats,
    Fine Bashan rams, high-quality wheat,
          and the blood of grapes: you drank good wine!

READ

Read the passage slowly and carefully, letting your mind dwell on the picture.

THINK

How would you summarize all of these images of God? What words describe these actions and metaphors? God never does the bare minimum needed for the work of redemption. When God seeks you, he will run through any desert and throw his arms around you. God not only provides what you need to survive — he gives lavishly, of the best quality that he has to offer. How have you seen the lavishness of God's provision in your life, when you thought you had nothing but the wilderness? How does your life reflect his generosity?

PRAY

Praise and thank God for your own personal examples of provision. Spend time specifically meditating on the lavishness of God's mercy; he has not only set you free, but guarded you jealously for himself.

LIVE

Write out your own images and metaphors about abundance. Is God spreading things before you like a wedding feast? Buying elaborately embroidered gowns? What shows you his attention?

_____

_____

_____

DAY 116

EXPANDED PASSAGE: PSALM 90

ONCE UPON A TIME

PSALM 90:1-2

1-2 God, it seems you've been our home forever;
   long before the mountains were born,
 Long before you brought earth itself to birth,
   from "once upon a time" to "kingdom come" — you are God.

READ

Read the passage slowly and carefully several times through.

THINK

When you hear the word *time*, what comes into your thoughts? Do you automatically think about antiaging creams, fighting a losing battle, or the frantic pace of life? Sometimes things like mountains or the ocean can stop our frantic flailings in their tracks — that sort of ancientness can give perspective. But God is the One who made the ancient mountains, who existed before the earth's crust and the distant, burning stars. He is the God of all time — the God of *your* time as well. Do you treat him as mightier, more powerful, and more important than time? Or are you tempted to serve the god of business instead?

PRAY

Confess to God whatever your skewed view of time is. Anything in your mind that operates as though God is not Master should not be given room to stand. Thank God for being present before the beginning of the world and for holding its destiny in his hands — and your destiny alongside of it. Ask for the courage to believe that he is truly sovereign.

LIVE

Whatever dominates your time today, remember that Jesus is Lord over it — able to bring all things to good no matter how much or how little time you have.

YOU DON'T KNOW ABOUT TOMORROW

JAMES 4:13-15

13-15 And now I have a word for you who brashly announce, "Today — at the latest, tomorrow — we're off to such and such a city for the year. We're going to start a business and make a lot of money." You don't know the first thing about tomorrow. You're nothing but a wisp of fog, catching a brief bit of sun before disappearing. Instead, make it a habit to say, "If the Master wills it and we're still alive, we'll do this or that."

READ

Read the passage slowly and carefully. Consider where you see yourself in this imagined conversation.

THINK

James is not afraid to lay out the harsh truth to his readers. On the surface, this might seem to be a passage about procrastination, but it is really much more than that. How often do you forget that God is the One who prospers your work, that he is the God of time itself? We might remember our mortality in a crash or with the sudden death of someone in our community, but to truly give each day back to God and see life as a gift is something we hardly seem to have *time* to do. Instead we rely on our own planning for purpose, our own vacations for rest, our own methods for health.

PRAY

Thank God for the gift of life today. Praise him for all that he has allowed you to do so far. Confess all the "plans" you have made without considering your dependence on him for life and prosperity. Ask God to endow you with a deep sense of your need for him. Ask for a heart of gratitude along the way.

LIVE

There is no promise of tomorrow. How does that change how you live today?

WORK WITH A FLOURISHING FINISH

PHILIPPIANS 1:3-6

3-6   Every time you cross my mind, I break out in exclamations of thanks to God. Each exclamation is a trigger to prayer. I find myself praying for you with a glad heart. I am so pleased that you have continued on in this with us, believing and proclaiming God's Message, from the day you heard it right up to the present. There has never been the slightest doubt in my mind that the God who started this great work in you would keep at it and bring it to a flourishing finish on the very day Christ Jesus appears.

READ

Read the passage slowly. As Paul speaks to his audience, think about to whom you might speak these words or who might speak them about you.

THINK

Have you ever been beset by unfinished tasks? Or even worse, has someone else's unfinished task shifted to become your responsibility? Sometimes it feels absolutely futile to keep working — like our hard efforts never quite produce "enough." The laundry keeps coming, the bills pile up, and our best plans get thwarted and delayed. But God does not have the same limitations. He does not forget or get too busy to achieve salvation. The mighty salvation work he has started is sustained by the same power that made the stars and keeps the earth spinning. Does that move you to gratitude? What sort of "completion" is God moving you toward?

PRAY

Praise and thank God for never giving up on his "work" in you. Ask God for a sense of faith and trust when it seems like you are just one big "under construction" zone. Pray for the courage to believe that God will not abandon you and has your greatest good in mind.

LIVE

Live today knowing that God will be faithful to complete the work of salvation he has started in you. Let that knowledge shape the way you view your own tasks — finished and unfinished. Live with thanks.

GOD IS ETERNAL

PSALM 103:15-18

15-18   Men and women don't live very long;
       like wildflowers they spring up and blossom,
    But a storm snuffs them out just as quickly,
       leaving nothing to show they were here.
    GOD's love, though, is ever and always,
       eternally present to all who fear him,
    Making everything right for them and their children
       as they follow his Covenant ways
       and remember to do whatever he said.

READ

Read the passage slowly and carefully. Try to picture the scene.

THINK

How do you picture your life? Something that you are building slowly, bit by bit? A big, empty canvas where you are distinguishing yourself from others? Something that seems to be full of a million tomorrows? This passage instead proclaims that our lives are fragile. They can be "snuffed out" as quickly as wildflowers in a terrible storm, leaving no trace behind. God's love lives forever. Those who depend on God's love rather than the "strength" of their own lives have lasting hope.

PRAY

Ask God to give you a sense of the fragility of your life that will not drive you to despair but instead push you to trust in God's love. Praise God for his love and goodness, which lasts beyond the lives of humans — going before and after your life on earth. Pray for reliance on his purpose and protection.

LIVE

Life is fragile and precious, valuable only based on the good gifts of God. Make sure that you are working toward the eternal today, because that outlasts the very uncertain "now."

STAY THE COURSE

JAMES 5:10-11

10-11   Take the old prophets as your mentors. They put up with anything, went through everything, and never once quit, all the time honoring God. What a gift life is to those who stay the course! You've heard, of course, of Job's staying power, and you know how God brought it all together for him at the end. That's because God cares, cares right down to the last detail.

READ

Read the passage slowly and carefully, considering all of the phrases. Pause. Read the passage slowly again.

THINK

Consider the stories of the prophets that you know. Do they seem like the type of people you would naturally gravitate toward as mentors? It's hard to imagine Elijah or John the Baptist oozing calming proverbs over a cup of tea. So why then does James suggest you take on those folks as your mentors? They knew how to endure, how to persevere, how to speak the truth regardless of the cost. Not only did they simply hang on, they managed to endure difficult circumstances in a way that brought glory to God. The point of taking on prophetic endurance is not just for the bragging rights of tough faith, however. Endurance has its beginning and ending in God's ability to end our stories beautifully.

PRAY

Ask God for the mentorship of endurance. Pray for the same spirit of determined praise that Job had — whether you are suffering a lot or a little in your life. Praise God for the care he has over every detail that allows you to respond trustfully in any situation.

LIVE

God cares down to the last detail. Live in faith, knowing that he works all things for your good. Endure all things with praise, even hardships.

A RISKY CALL

ACTS 9:10-17

10   There was a disciple in Damascus by the name of Ananias. The Master spoke to him in a vision: "Ananias."

"Yes, Master?" he answered.

11-12   "Get up and go over to Straight Avenue. Ask at the house of Judas for a man from Tarsus. His name is Saul. He's there praying. He has just had a dream in which he saw a man named Ananias enter the house and lay hands on him so he could see again."

13-14   Ananias protested, "Master, you can't be serious. Everybody's talking about this man and the terrible things he's been doing, his reign of terror against your people in Jerusalem! And now he's shown up here with papers from the Chief Priest that give him license to do the same to us."

15-16   But the Master said, "Don't argue. Go! I have picked him as my personal representative to non-Jews and kings and Jews. And now I'm about to show him what he's in for — the hard suffering that goes with this job."

17   So Ananias went and found the house, placed his hands on blind Saul, and said, "Brother Saul, the Master sent me, the same Jesus you saw on your way here. He sent me so you could see again and be filled with the Holy Spirit."

READ

Read the passage aloud. Try to imagine the emotions and actions of the scene.

THINK

Can you imagine yourself in Ananias's shoes? God seems to be telling him to turn himself in. Notice that God's command doesn't say, "Don't worry — I'm going to keep him tied up." God not only sends Ananias to a dangerous enemy of the church — he sends him to heal him. And Saul isn't even going to come to Ananias — *he* has to seek out the street and the house where Saul will be found! After his initial concern, we see Ananias's obedience. Not only does he do what he is told, he calls Saul "brother." How do you respond when the call of God is inconvenient, dangerous, seemingly contradictory? Who seems beyond God's reach? Might God be calling you to reach out to them?

PRAY

Ask for the Spirit of God to fill you. Listen for the call of God. Whatever inconvenient, difficult task God has called you to, pray for the courage to trust God's purposes for that person and for you. Thank God for using even those who oppose him for his purposes through grace.

LIVE

Journal about what your initial response would be if you were in Ananias's place. Then journal about your concerns and anxieties about the calls God has placed in your life.

_____

_____

_____

EVERYTHING NEW

REVELATION 21:2-5

2 I saw Holy Jerusalem, new-created, descending resplendent out of Heaven, as ready for God as a bride for her husband.

3-5 I heard a voice thunder from the Throne: "Look! Look! God has moved into the neighborhood, making his home with men and women! They're his people, he's their God. He'll wipe every tear from their eyes. Death is gone for good — tears gone, crying gone, pain gone — all the first order of things gone." The Enthroned continued, "Look! I'm making everything new. Write it all down — each word dependable and accurate."

READ

Read the passage slowly and carefully. Imagine the thunderous, authoritative voice. Read the passage again, pausing after each phrase, each significant word.

THINK

In this vision of Paradise, the voice from the Throne commands John to "look." What does the voice urge him to observe? God's presence is among his people, finally, completely, and wholly in a way that was only hinted at in human history. Death is gone — tears are gone. Pain has disappeared. All things are being made new. Can you imagine the glistening joy of a world without pain, a world where God is with his people, constantly and visibly present? Although this is in many ways the promise of the future, this is also the kingdom you have already inherited — *today.* Jesus proclaimed that this kingdom was here with his arrival, even while we wait for his second coming. The work of making all things new starts with *you* — the new life that Jesus has given to you by his work of salvation. How does this make you feel?

PRAY

Ask God for glimpses of this new creation and the ways it is already at work in your life and the world around you. Praise and thank Jesus for getting rid of the old, for conquering death, and for experiencing pain on our behalf so we could walk into Paradise. Pray for the joy that comes from this sense of God's kingdom to flood into your life as surely as if you stepped into the new creation today.

LIVE

Journal about something in your life that you have already seen God make new — grief and tears wiped away, a healed wound, or something else that rings with the promise of Paradise.

_____

_____

_____

STANDING TALL IN HIS BRIGHT PRESENCE

JUDE 24-25

24-25 And now to him who can keep you on your feet, standing tall in his bright presence, fresh and celebrating — to our one God, our only Savior, through Jesus Christ, our Master, be glory, majesty, strength, and rule before all time, and now, and to the end of all time. Yes.

READ

Read this short passage carefully, considering how it characterizes us and God.

THINK

Does it ever feel like you can hardly stand on your own? Do you ever feel so emotionally or physically exhausted it seems a struggle to climb to your feet in the morning? No matter how impossible that task seems to you, it is not an impossible task to God. He is able to keep you "on your feet" and to keep you from falling—whether that means fighting the good fight of the faith, working for his glory, raising a family, or simply taking the step forward that you need to receive help. In his presence, God can make you "fresh" and clean, sinless and joyful. Who is doing the work of keeping you pure and on your feet here? It is not you. Instead, it is the powerful, mighty, and merciful Jesus who had glory, majesty, and strength before time even began. He is the one in charge of keeping you upright. Take heart.

PRAY

Praise God for his power and might, which created the universe and can keep you going when nothing else can. Thank him for his salvation, which presents you "fresh" to God. Ask for the courage to believe that he will keep you on your feet and keep you from falling.

LIVE

God can keep you on your feet, and it is not because of your own efforts or qualities, but instead his infinite mercy. Walk forward and don't be afraid of falling. He will catch you.

WASHED BY THE SPIRIT

TITUS 3:3-8

3-8 It wasn't so long ago that we ourselves were stupid and stubborn, dupes of sin, ordered every which way by our glands, going around with a chip on our shoulder, hated and hating back. But when God, our kind and loving Savior God, stepped in, he saved us from all that. It was all his doing; we had nothing to do with it. He gave us a good bath, and we came out of it new people, washed inside and out by the Holy Spirit. Our Savior Jesus poured out new life so generously. God's gift has restored our relationship with him and given us back our lives. And there's more life to come — an eternity of life! You can count on this.

READ

Read the passage slowly and carefully, pondering the process described.

THINK

When you think of sin, do you think of a dark, overwhelmingly evil force? While sin is indeed a force to reckon with, on what level is it simply "stupid"? Think about some "stupid sins" you've committed or that you have seen needlessly wreck the lives of others. When you see sin for what it is — absurd rebellion against a God who never picked a fight — it becomes revealed in all of its silliness. What becomes even more evident is that despite the stupidity, we cannot seem to break free. How does God come into the picture? Can you visualize him, like a parent, cleaning the sticky mess off of a child hopelessly dirty? What do you think it means that God has "given us back our lives"?

PRAY

Ask for the Holy Spirit to reveal the ways in which you are a dupe of sin — your fears, your insecurities, your petty and repetitive behaviors. Pray for the power of Christ to fill you so that you can break free — not under your own strength, but because God has already cleansed you and claimed you as his own. Ask for true life, not simply slipping back into the motions of "stupid" sin.

LIVE

Write about the stupidity of sin as you've seen it in your life and the ways in which God has given you your life back as you have left sins behind.

_____

_____

_____

NO SPIRITUAL FLABBINESS, PLEASE!

1 TIMOTHY 4:6-10

6-10 You've been raised on the Message of the faith and have followed sound teaching. Now pass on this counsel to the followers of Jesus there, and you'll be a good servant of Jesus. Stay clear of silly stories that get dressed up as religion. Exercise daily in God—no spiritual flabbiness, please! Workouts in the gymnasium are useful, but a disciplined life in God is far more so, making you fit both today and forever. You can count on this. Take it to heart. This is why we've thrown ourselves into this venture so totally. We're banking on the living God, Savior of all men and women, especially believers.

READ

Read the passage carefully and slowly, attentive to tone. What "teaching pictures" does Paul use?

THINK

Exercise consumes our culture, especially as women. Mostly, we are tempted to focus on which exercises will trim our thighs, flatten our tummies, and otherwise perfect what we see as flawed. Maybe when we get it right it becomes about health and not appearance — about feeling your heart pumping blood to your legs, the satisfaction of burning legs and stretching muscles. And yet that investment will inevitably die with our bodies. Discipline and health, however, are a picture of what we should be striving for with God. In what ways does "spiritual flabbiness" kick in? Is "spiritual exercise" tempting because of how it appears to others as well? What sort of "health" do you think Paul is encouraging here?

PRAY

Journal a prayer unique to the idea of "spiritual exercise." Ask God for the greater health that you need.

_____

_____

_____

LIVE

Today, take a small step toward greater spiritual health. Don't try to change everything at once, like a New Year's resolution doomed to fail. Make one small move and be consistent.

GIVE DIGNITY TO YOUR BODY

1 THESSALONIANS 4:4-5

4-5   Learn to appreciate and give dignity to your body, not abusing it, as is so common among those who know nothing of God.

READ

Read this short passage carefully. It is packed with significance.

THINK

Many in the ancient world considered the body a shell, a prison — simply an external, cumbersome thing that traps the soul. While we might feel that way in the case of illness or exhaustion, Christians hold to the doctrine that God made the body good — something to encompass our souls and yet so much more than simply a container. Why do you think God wants us to appreciate and give dignity to our bodies? How might that be different from forcing them to look the way we want them to look? What does it mean to abuse the body, especially in modern culture? Knowing God should make us act differently toward our bodies. As a woman, why is it so difficult to appreciate and give dignity to your body?

PRAY

Ask God for guidance and discernment in how you can appreciate and give dignity to your body. While it might seem a small "surface" thing, your body is a big part of your life. Ask for humble trust in God's design for every molecule of you.

LIVE

Journal about the ways in which culture encourages abuse of the body, and ponder why that is a symptom of not understanding or knowing God.

_____

_____

_____

LIVING FREELY

GALATIANS 5:16-18

16-18 My counsel is this: Live freely, animated and motivated by God's Spirit. Then you won't feed the compulsions of selfishness. For there is a root of sinful self-interest in us that is at odds with a free spirit, just as the free spirit is incompatible with selfishness. These two ways of life are antithetical, so that you cannot live at times one way and at times another way according to how you feel on any given day. Why don't you choose to be led by the Spirit and so escape the erratic compulsions of a law-dominated existence?

READ

Read this section through carefully and observantly. Read it aloud again.

THINK

Paul spends most of his letter to the Galatians encouraging them to pursue true freedom rather than the legalism they had labeled as spirituality. In this passage, however, he makes an important distinction between freedom and free-for-all living. Our culture places a lot of value in freedom — as a right, as a lifestyle, as a rebellion against rules that seem oppressive or just plain wrong. How is freedom defined in Christ? What is the purpose of the freedom you have received from the gospel? Paul encourages a lack of legalism, not a lack of love. He describes the Spirit leading to a kind of freedom that is not sporadic, but constantly working toward greater love and selflessness. Have you properly understood the purpose of your freedom? Do you need greater freedom from the "compulsions of selfishness" that often disguise themselves as freedom?

PRAY

Ask God for the true freedom that he gives — not only freedom from fear and legalism, but also freedom from a lifestyle of self. Pray for the Spirit to guide you toward steady, trustworthy freedom. Ask for specific ways to resist the selfishness that tempts you and to instead pursue "animated" living that will bring growth and health.

LIVE

With freedom comes certain burdens. Consider before God your use of time and your investment in relationships. Use your freedom for the good of others and watch as your freedom increases tenfold.

GOD OVER JERICHO

JOSHUA 2:3-13

3 The king of Jericho sent word to Rahab: "Bring out the men who came to you to stay the night in your house. They're spies: they've come to spy out the whole country."

4-7 The woman had taken the two men and hidden them. She said, "Yes, two men did come to me, but I didn't know where they'd come from. At dark, when the gate was about to be shut, the men left. But I have no idea where they went. Hurry up! Chase them — you can still catch them!" (She had actually taken them up on the roof and hidden them under the stalks of flax that were spread out for her on the roof.) So the men set chase down the Jordan road toward the fords. As soon as they were gone, the gate was shut.

8-11 Before the spies were down for the night, the woman came up to them on the roof and said, "I know that GOD has given you the land. We're all afraid. Everyone in the country feels hopeless. We heard how GOD dried up the waters of the Red Sea before you when you left Egypt, and what he did to the two Amorite kings east of the Jordan, Sihon and Og, whom you put under a holy curse and destroyed. We heard it and our hearts sank. We all had the wind knocked out of us. And all because of you, you and GOD, your God, God of the heavens above and God of the earth below.

12-13 "Now promise me by GOD. I showed you mercy; now show my family mercy. And give me some tangible proof, a guarantee of life for my father and mother, my brothers and sisters — everyone connected with my family. Save our souls from death!"

READ

Read the passage, trying to imagine all of the sights, sounds, and smells of the scene. What were the emotions running through each character? Picture the blood pounding in their veins, the night sky. What is at stake?

THINK

What motivates Rahab? The king of her entire nation asks for her cooperation and she denies it. Why? Reexamine verses 8-11. What power does she recognize as more important even than loyalty to her country and her people? Do you recognize the authority of God as such an overwhelming force in your own life? What would you need to do to realign your service to be to the God of the universe first?

PRAY

Ask God to reveal the "Jerichos" in your own life — the things that lay hold of your loyalty and seem to have the most power and influence over your fate. Pray for the wisdom to realign your loyalty to God alone, so that, if necessary, you will do things that might seem to contradict your duties.

LIVE

Journal about what you think might have been going through Rahab's mind as she decided to hide the spies. Use first-person if it is helpful, and include a meditation on this God you have heard of as a distant and mighty conqueror.

_____

_____

_____

A VOICE OF MERCY

2 KINGS 5:1-4

1-3   Naaman was general of the army under the king of Aram. He was important to his master, who held him in the highest esteem because it was by him that GOD had given victory to Aram: a truly great man, but afflicted with a grievous skin disease. It so happened that Aram, on one of its raiding expeditions against Israel, captured a young girl who became a maid to Naaman's wife. One day she said to her mistress, "Oh, if only my master could meet the prophet of Samaria, he would be healed of his skin disease."

4   Naaman went straight to his master and reported what the girl from Israel had said.

READ

Imagine yourself as a young girl, far from home, enslaved by your enemies and separated from your family. Ponder how you might think of your masters, especially if one was ill. Then, read this passage slowly aloud.

THINK

The servant girl, who remains unnamed, was in a position about as oppressive as you can imagine. As a woman in a foreign land and a slave, her "voice" was incredibly small, her power almost imperceptible. Did she hesitate to speak? Was this a moment when she broke through a usually silent and respectful demeanor, taking a risk to mention the prophet? We will never know. What we do know, however, is that this one recorded instance of her voice expressed mercy—a desire for healing for the ones who had hurt her country and personally harmed her. Although far from home, her thoughts were on Israel's God, Israel's prophets, and their power even to heal her "enemies."

PRAY

Write a prayer asking for healing for someone who has oppressed or harmed you, whether in an overt way or in small and subtle ways.

_____

_____

_____

LIVE

Now more than ever, women have a voice in society. We are encouraged to be strong and proud, calling out any oppression we might see. Instead of using your voice to denounce those who hurt you or extol your own cleverness, use your voice to proclaim God's power and healing. If this servant girl far from home used her small speech for forgiveness, how much more your own voice, in your own home?

DON'T FAKE IT

ROMANS 12:9-13

9-10   Love from the center of who you are; don't fake it. Run for dear life from evil; hold on for dear life to good. Be good friends who love deeply; practice playing second fiddle.

11-13   Don't burn out; keep yourselves fueled and aflame. Be alert servants of the Master, cheerfully expectant. Don't quit in hard times; pray all the harder. Help needy Christians; be inventive in hospitality.

READ

Read the passage carefully, pausing after each sentence and phrase to truly take in the message. Read the passage through again, trying to perceive how each phrase connects to the next one.

THINK

As women especially, our culture expects us to be "nice." Sometimes the church takes this cultural expectation of fake cheerfulness and multiplies it tenfold. We can become so trained to avoid conflict that instead of being loving, we end up being merely polite. Words are one of the most wonderful and dangerous tools women have. To "love from the center of who you are" means a lot more than simply being "nice." It means being open, honest, and genuine—which means asking for forgiveness and giving it, expressing your insecurities and carefully addressing those of others instead of cashing in on them. What needs to happen for you to go from being a "nice" lady to one who "loves deeply"?

PRAY

Confess honestly the areas where you have faked it and fallen short of loving. Ask God for his Spirit to move you toward genuine, deep love for others that is not content with appearances alone.

LIVE

Journal honestly about the relationships and situations in which you are the most tempted to fake it. What pressures you to put on an appearance of love? How can you ask God for help in becoming more genuinely loving? What do you need in order for that to occur?

TRUE FREEDOM

GALATIANS 5:19-21

19-21 It is obvious what kind of life develops out of trying to get your own way all the time: repetitive, loveless, cheap sex; a stinking accumulation of mental and emotional garbage; frenzied and joyless grabs for happiness; trinket gods; magic-show religion; paranoid loneliness; cutthroat competition; all-consuming-yet-never-satisfied wants; a brutal temper; an impotence to love or be loved; divided homes and divided lives; small-minded and lopsided pursuits; the vicious habit of depersonalizing everyone into a rival; uncontrolled and uncontrollable addictions; ugly parodies of community. I could go on.

This isn't the first time I have warned you, you know. If you use your freedom this way, you will not inherit God's kingdom.

READ

Read the passage through very slowly. Pause after each idea on the list, considering each word.

THINK

If you see nothing on this list that sounds like a part of the deep, dark portions of your heart, you are probably not considering yourself very honestly. Not only is this the kind of life that you naturally gravitate toward because of your sinful nature, this is the kind of life our culture applauds and encourages. How does your desire to live your own way lead particularly to one or more of these terrible sins? What items on this list are especially tempting or common for women in the modern world? How about for men? In what ways is this behavior a perversion of the free will God has given humanity?

PRAY

Confess to God all of the sins that you have been convicted of through this passage — general attitudes as well as specific actions. Pray for God to reveal the emptiness of these patterns to you, and ask that your life be one characterized by avoiding these all-too-common behaviors. Pray also for the women around you — for wisdom, health, and confidence in Christ's true freedom, which helps to combat these empty pursuits.

LIVE

Journal about three specific phrases that convicted you from this passage of Scripture and the ways in which you can address them today. Consider Christ's power as the resource for this, not your own strength.

HANDS FULL OR HANDS EMPTY

PHILIPPIANS 4:11-13

11-13 Actually, I don't have a sense of needing anything personally. I've learned by now to be quite content whatever my circumstances. I'm just as happy with little as with much, with much as with little. I've found the recipe for being happy whether full or hungry, hands full or hands empty. Whatever I have, wherever I am, I can make it through anything in the One who makes me who I am.

READ

Read Paul's words to the Philippians aloud. What seems to be the tone? What emotion do you imagine running through this passage?

THINK

How many times do you find yourself postponing happiness? Rest? Relationships? It is easy to say that when this or that is over, you will be happy. But Jesus does not present goal-oriented joy or happiness based on unlocking achievements. The precursor to the often-quoted verse "I can do all things through Christ who strengthens me" is this easily overlooked section on contentment — the very foundation of what it means to do all things. What do you think is the happiness that Paul is referring to — is it an absence of troubles or difficulties? Or some way of adjusting in the midst of them?

PRAY

Confess to God all of the conditions that you have put on having un-- limited, always-present contentment. Ask the Spirit to reveal to you the ingratitude or anxiety that is standing between you and a sense of deep peace and happiness. Ask for the consistent joy that God gives instead of conditional and fading "success" achieved on your own. Pray for the eyes to see how much has been given to you.

LIVE

Search your memory and journal about a time when you have had very little but yet been very content. How was the Lord present in those circumstances? How does that speak to your present anxiety?

HE WILL KEEP YOU ON TRACK

PROVERBS 3:5-7

5-7 Trust GOD from the bottom of your heart;
   don't try to figure out everything on your own.
  Listen for GOD's voice in everything you do, everywhere you go;
   he's the one who will keep you on track.
  Don't assume that you know it all.
   Run to GOD! Run from evil!

READ

Pause for a few moments in silence, praying for wisdom before you read these words about wisdom. Then read the passage slowly aloud.

THINK

What makes you so desperate to figure everything out on your own? The desire for rationality, for control and order out of chaos, is not bad in itself. Our culture urges us to be independent, strong, and not burden others. So, what is the problem with relying solely on yourself for life direction? It is that in your sinful self-reliance God's good plan is lost in fear and self-deceptions. In this world full of noise that "directs" you, both inwardly and outwardly, what do you think it means to truly listen for God's voice and to trust that he directs your path?

PRAY

Spend time "listening" in prayer. Lay before God the many paths and their perils. Ask for wisdom and clear direction in the best route to take — whether a big decision or a seemingly small one. Spend a portion of your prayer time in silence.

LIVE

Journal about when you have seen God direct you along a path, or journal about the substance of what you "heard" today in your prayer time. How has and is God directing you?

_____

_____

_____

DARING DEVOTION

2 SAMUEL 23:13-17

13-17   One day during harvest, the Three parted from the Thirty and joined David at the Cave of Adullam. A squad of Philistines had set up camp in the Valley of Rephaim. While David was holed up in the Cave, the Philistines had their base camp in Bethlehem. David had a sudden craving and said, "Would I ever like a drink of water from the well at the gate of Bethlehem!" So the Three penetrated the Philistine lines, drew water from the well at the gate of Bethlehem, and brought it back to David. But David wouldn't drink it; he poured it out as an offering to GOD, saying, "There is no way, GOD, that I'll drink this! This isn't mere water, it's their life-blood—they risked their very lives to bring it!" So David refused to drink it.

This is the sort of thing that the Three did.

READ

As you read this story about David's Mighty Men, visualize the sights, sounds, and smells, and enter the emotions of this story.

THINK

The love of their king was so strong in these three men that they overheard a wish, a whim really, and risked their lives to bring it about. They heard (or overheard?) David's desire and didn't wait for a command, if it would ever have come. They were so desirous of pleasing their king that even David recognized it for what it truly was—an echo of the deepest kind of service and devotion that we should give to God. As a woman, you probably won't be hefting any swords in the near future to sate a king's thirst—but is there another sort of battle that you would take on, fueled simply by love for your King Jesus?

PRAY

Write a confession about the things that stop you from this sort of love. Ask God to reveal the desires of his heart and for the courage to pursue them out of love.

_____

_____

_____

LIVE

Do whatever must be done for the sake of love. Don't be afraid of enemy lines or being outnumbered—to seek the will of God is always the safest course.

ADVENTUROUSLY EXPECTANT

ROMANS 8:15-17

15-17   This resurrection life you received from God is not a timid, grave-tending life. It's adventurously expectant, greeting God with a childlike "What's next, Papa?" God's Spirit touches our spirits and confirms who we really are. We know who he is, and we know who we are: Father and children. And we know we are going to get what's coming to us — an unbelievable inheritance! We go through exactly what Christ goes through. If we go through the hard times with him, then we're certainly going to go through the good times with him!

READ

As you read, visualize the example that Paul gives, using what you know of a child's perspective. Let it overtake your imagination for a moment.

THINK

More and more in our culture, the image of "father" has baggage attached to it. More often than ever before, it seems that fathers are absent and avoiding leadership, leaving many moms to try to fill every part of the parenting role. Whatever your experience with fathers, however, try to latch onto what Paul is saying. This Father will never leave, never be tempted, never be distant or hard to know. In the best circumstances, children in their father's company become both bold and submissive, adventurous and yet perfectly safe and comfortable. Our Father "confirms who we really are" — which means you don't need to be anything more than a child, at ease and curious about the world. Nothing can harm you, not even hard times, because your Father's inheritance is coming to *you*. The Creator of the universe is your family. Why not go out and explore in gratitude? He is with you!

PRAY

Confess before God all of the things that keep you from being a child in his presence. Come clean about the timidity that makes you anxious. Ask for a sense of his presence, his protection, and his unfailing love. Pray for an "adventurous" spirit as you go out into the world, eager to do his will and comfortable with your own shortcomings and his supplemental strength.

LIVE

Journal about the kind of Father God is and how you can enter into your role as his child. If it is helpful, explore the contrast between your own earthly father and God, especially if you think that keeps you from entering into your spiritual role as a childlike receiver.

IS ANYTHING TOO HARD FOR GOD?

GENESIS 18:9-15

9 The men said to him, "Where is Sarah your wife?"

He said, "In the tent."

10 One of them said, "I'm coming back about this time next year. When I arrive, your wife Sarah will have a son." Sarah was listening at the tent opening, just behind the man.

11-12 Abraham and Sarah were old by this time, very old. Sarah was far past the age for having babies. Sarah laughed within herself, "An old woman like me? Get pregnant? With this old man of a husband?"

13-14 GOD said to Abraham, "Why did Sarah laugh saying, 'Me? Have a baby? An old woman like me?' Is anything too hard for GOD? I'll be back about this time next year and Sarah will have a baby."

15 Sarah lied. She said, "I didn't laugh," because she was afraid.

But he said, "Yes you did; you laughed."

READ

Read the passage slowly and carefully, trying to imagine the sights, sounds, and emotions of the scene. How did Sarah's emotions change throughout the text?

THINK

Whatever drives Sarah to listen at the tent opening, she seems astonished to hear her name on the stranger's lips. Do you think her laugh is disbelief? Skepticism? The bitter laugh of disappointment? The key to this passage is that she laughed "within herself" — that deep-down despair that we all sometimes know but rarely share. Yet God *knew* that she laughed — and asked the rhetorical question, "Is anything too hard for GOD?" Of course she seems afraid that God knew of her response and tries to deny it — but the mighty God knows her through and through — her doubts, her disappointment, her grief, and her disbelief—and he will not let her off the hook. His power is stronger than her disappointment.

PRAY

What things has God promised that make you laugh or question deep within yourself? Write a prayer of confession about the specific promises you feel God has given, yet you feel uncertain. Don't try to hide your deep emotions from him.

_____

_____

_____

LIVE

Is anything too hard for God? Doubt is comfortable and, more than ever, cynicism and skepticism are more fashionable than hope. Let this question resound over all of the uncertainties in your life; let it take root deeper than all of your disappointments. Nothing is too hard, no time frame too tight, no physical factors of the universe too overwhelming, for God to accomplish his purposes.

A VOICE OF JUSTICE

JUDGES 4:4-9

4-5 Deborah was a prophet, the wife of Lappidoth. She was judge over Israel at that time. She held court under Deborah's Palm between Ramah and Bethel in the hills of Ephraim. The People of Israel went to her in matters of justice.

6-7 She sent for Barak son of Abinoam from Kedesh in Naphtali and said to him, "It has become clear that GOD, the God of Israel, commands you: Go to Mount Tabor and prepare for battle. Take ten companies of soldiers from Naphtali and Zebulun. I'll take care of getting Sisera, the leader of Jabin's army, to the Kishon River with all his chariots and troops. And I'll make sure you win the battle."

8 Barak said, "If you go with me, I'll go. But if you don't go with me, I won't go."

9 She said, "Of course I'll go with you. But understand that with an attitude like that, there'll be no glory in it for you. GOD will use a woman's hand to take care of Sisera."

READ

Read the passage slowly and carefully. Imagine Deborah and her place in the community. What dynamics do you notice as Deborah interacts with others?

THINK

Deborah is a prophetess. Scholars have debated for many years what exactly that title means in this context, but regardless of the specific "job description," she is seen as a leader. People come to her for "matters of justice," so they must perceive her as unbiased and wise. Based on her command to Barak, she has a clear sense of God's will. She is a clarifier and a coordinator. How does her attitude seem to contrast Barak's? What aspects of Deborah's leadership would you like to imitate in your own life?

PRAY

Ask God to form you into a woman of justice — someone who is known as being fair and certain of his will, not for your own reputation, but to prove his power. If you find yourself siding more with Barak, wanting a "security blanket," ask for a greater faith and understanding of God's will of victory. Confess the things that keep you from leadership, wherever you are called to it.

LIVE

Journal about the ways in which God has called you to leadership. Although it may not be a visible or obvious position, how are you called to be clarifying and coordinating in your family? In your job? In your church community? Write how you can pursue justice and fair-mindedness.

YOU BELONG HERE

EPHESIANS 2:19-22

19-22 That's plain enough, isn't it? You're no longer wandering exiles. This kingdom of faith is now your home country. You're no longer strangers or outsiders. You *belong* here, with as much right to the name Christian as anyone. God is building a home. He's using us all — irrespective of how we got here — in what he is building. He used the apostles and prophets for the foundation. Now he's using you, fitting you in brick by brick, stone by stone, with Christ Jesus as the cornerstone that holds all the parts together. We see it taking shape day after day — a holy temple built by God, all of us built into it, a temple in which God is quite at home.

READ

Visualize a grand and beautiful building. Slowly read this passage, allowing Paul's metaphor to wash over you. What do you notice and observe about the passage?

THINK

How does the world assign identity to you? Do you only feel valuable sometimes in terms of who you're married to, how well your children do in school, or whether or not you live up to the expectations of others? No wonder we often end up feeling like "exiles" — like our identity is confused or conditional. But clearly, that is not the case. No matter how much you used to wander, searching for something to define you, you now have purpose. You are part of a beautiful building — and not a spare part either. How valuable do you think you are to God in order to be a part of the home that God is building? Could that value possibly depend on you, or could it disappear?

PRAY

Lay before God all of the things, past and present, that make you feel like a wanderer or an exile. Thank him for not leaving you outside but instead making you an essential part of his plan. Ask God for a daily sense of identity in him that is as enduring as stone. Pray for the eyes to see that you are "at home" no matter where you are or what has happened to you.

LIVE

Journal about the places in your life where it has become evident you are no longer on the outside. Where do you feel the most "at home" in God's plan? Where is it the most evident that you are part of the home that God is building?

_____

_____

_____

SUCH A TIME AS THIS

ESTHER 4:12-14

12-14 When Hathach told Mordecai what Esther had said, Mordecai sent her this message: "Don't think that just because you live in the king's house you're the one Jew who will get out of this alive. If you persist in staying silent at a time like this, help and deliverance will arrive for the Jews from someplace else; but you and your family will be wiped out. Who knows? Maybe you were made queen for just such a time as this."

READ

Recall what you can of the story of Esther. Read this moment of crisis and climax as freshly as you can, trying to imagine yourself in Mordecai's desperate position and Esther's dangerous position.

THINK

Because we know the end of the story, you might tend to think of Esther as a strong and courageous person—and she was. But first, she was a young woman out of her element, with danger all around her. The society she was in was biased against her as a woman and prejudiced against her Jewish heritage. Instead of jumping ship when Haman convinces the king to wipe out the Jews, however, Esther carefully finds a way to walk the balance—she claims solidarity with her past and her people while also honoring her commitment to the king. Mordecai, instead of twisting her arm, is confident that God will save his people no matter what. However, she has the option—perhaps she was put in her unique position for the purpose of giving a voice to the voiceless. Is that something that maybe God is doing in your own life?

PRAY

Ask God to reveal the "such a time as this" space within your own life. Journal a prayer of confession and petition, inviting God to make clear your unique position and his special saving will. Be open to what he shows you in this time.

_____

_____

_____

LIVE

139

Whether in your work or your friendships, your marriage or your church community, God has given you your unique background, skill set, and positioning for specific reasons. Thank him for working redemption. Thank him for inviting you to be a part of that process, and ask for the courage to step forward into whatever he has laid out to you.

ACCEPT THE HELP

HEBREWS 4:14-16

14-16 Now that we know what we have — Jesus, this great High Priest with ready access to God — let's not let it slip through our fingers. We don't have a priest who is out of touch with our reality. He's been through weakness and testing, experienced it all — all but the sin. So let's walk right up to him and get what he is so ready to give. Take the mercy, accept the help.

READ

Read the passage slowly and carefully. Pause after each sentence. Then read the passage aloud again.

THINK

Journal about a time, past or present, when you feel like others are out of touch with you — not understanding or unable to sympathize with your pain. Write about deep wounds that have been inflicted on you. Then take some time to consider that Jesus has felt all of those emotions — without sin.

_____

_____

_____

PRAY

Thank Jesus for a solidarity that goes beyond the deepest friends. Praise him for not leaving you isolated in misunderstanding. Knowing how very *with you* he is, ask for what you need. God's work is increased by your dependence and by your confidence in him. Pray for a spirit of trust in his generosity that goes beyond sharing wounds and extends into healing them.

LIVE

Women often seem to feel they have to hide their wounds to appear strong. There might be some fear in your life about appearing needy or burdensome. But the confidence suggested in this passage comes from knowing that not only are you needy, but that Jesus has met those needs and experienced those wounds alongside you. Be bold and dependent on Christ. The two do not cancel each other out.

CARING FROM THE CROSS

JOHN 19:23-30

23-24 When they crucified him, the Roman soldiers took his clothes and divided them up four ways, to each soldier a fourth. But his robe was seamless, a single piece of weaving, so they said to each other, "Let's not tear it up. Let's throw dice to see who gets it." This confirmed the Scripture that said, "They divided up my clothes among them and threw dice for my coat." (The soldiers validated the Scriptures!)

24-27 While the soldiers were looking after themselves, Jesus' mother, his aunt, Mary the wife of Clopas, and Mary Magdalene stood at the foot of the cross. Jesus saw his mother and the disciple he loved standing near her. He said to his mother, "Woman, here is your son." Then to the disciple, "Here is your mother." From that moment the disciple accepted her as his own mother.

28 Jesus, seeing that everything had been completed so that the Scripture record might also be complete, then said, "I'm thirsty."

29-30 A jug of sour wine was standing by. Someone put a sponge soaked with the wine on a javelin and lifted it to his mouth. After he took the wine, Jesus said, "It's done . . . complete." Bowing his head, he offered up his spirit.

READ

Picture the setting of this exchange. Enter into the emotions that must have been running through each character's mind as the conversation progresses.

THINK

For Mary to show up at her son's site of execution must have been one of the most painful events of her life. What do you think drew her? What do you think she felt? In the midst of her powerlessness, in the midst of her own terrible grief, Jesus still provides for her, even while enduring his own unspeakable pain. This is the way God cares for his family, which includes you. He does not promise that there will be constant happiness. He does promise his presence in the midst of grief. He does not promise there will be no loss in your life, but he does promise his divine and complete provision.

PRAY

Praise God for his provision no matter how difficult your circumstances. Thank him for specific ways that he has provided for you even in the midst of loss and grief. Pause to consider how deeply he cares for you.

LIVE

Journal about the great compassion of God, as you have seen it in your own life and in the lives of others.

_____

_____

_____

TAKE HEART AND GAIN STRENGTH

HABAKKUK 3:17-19

17-19   Though the cherry trees don't blossom
       And the strawberries don't ripen,
Though the apples are worm-eaten
       and the wheat fields stunted,
Though the sheep pens are sheepless
       and the cattle barns empty,
I'm singing joyful praise to God.
       I'm turning cartwheels of joy to my Savior GOD.
Counting on GOD's Rule to prevail,
       I take heart and gain strength.
I run like a deer.
       I feel like I'm king of the mountain!

READ

Read this passage slowly and carefully, focusing on all of the images and the tone of this poetry.

THINK

While you might not be dependent on farm crops for survival like the writer here, you can certainly think of a time when emptiness and ruin seemed to surround you on all sides. This is a passage focusing on hopes that were not fulfilled, bounty turned to desperation, abundance turned to loss. And yet, this speaker rejoices. Why and how is joy still present? How can counting on God's rule help you maintain joy? How do you respond to your own setbacks and losses?

PRAY

Praise God for his rule, which is never thwarted or set back. Thank God that he is at work even when external circumstances seem to suggest abadonment or destruction. Confess to God the way your responses fall short of joy in the midst of hard times. Ask the Lord to help you count on his kingdom and rule, and ask for the courage and strength you need from this source.

LIVE

Although you are called to be joyful even when things go wrong, you are not called to be inhuman or insensible to grief. Today, no matter what wheat fields have turned out stunted, know that you are not called to ignore your emotional difficulties, but instead to trust that even those will yield to God's plan. Don't turn a blind eye to your troubles or those of others — trust that God is at work even through them.

HIS GRACE IS ENOUGH

2 CORINTHIANS 12:8-10

8-10 At first I didn't think of it as a gift, and begged God to remove it. Three times I did that, and then he told me,

> My grace is enough; it's all you need.
> My strength comes into its own in your weakness.

Once I heard that, I was glad to let it happen. I quit focusing on the handicap and began appreciating the gift. It was a case of Christ's strength moving in on my weakness. Now I take limitations in stride, and with good cheer, these limitations that cut me down to size — abuse, accidents, opposition, bad breaks. I just let Christ take over! And so the weaker I get, the stronger I become.

READ

Read this passage slowly and carefully, pausing after each sentence to consider how one idea leads to the next.

THINK

There is so much pressure in our culture to be a "strong" woman. You might sometimes feel pulled in a thousand different directions — as a mother, daughter, friend, churchmember, wife — you are somehow supposed to be organized, productive, fit, service-oriented, and so much more. Paul was pulled down low by God with an unknown weakness just so he would know it wasn't about him. God is all that is needed — and in fact, God often works better when we're falling apart than when we're together. When you are in need of grace, God shines brightest. It becomes about his ability and not your image.

PRAY

Take some time to confess the weaknesses you have been resentful of. Whether physical, emotional, circumstantial, or relational, consider the fact that God might have orchestrated your biggest "flaws" to teach you a lesson of dependence. Thank God for making his power perfect not in spite of, but through, your frailty. Praise God for a strength that is not at all dependent on what you do or fail to do.

LIVE

Journal about one way in which you feel pressured, internally or externally, to be a strong woman. How does this passage bring those ideas into the gospel light? What does a strong woman really look like according to this passage?

STANDING TOGETHER

EXODUS 17:10-13

10-13 Joshua did what Moses ordered in order to fight Amalek. And Moses, Aaron, and Hur went to the top of the hill. It turned out that whenever Moses raised his hands, Israel was winning, but whenever he lowered his hands, Amalek was winning. But Moses' hands got tired. So they got a stone and set it under him. He sat on it and Aaron and Hur held up his hands, one on each side. So his hands remained steady until the sun went down. Joshua defeated Amalek and its army in battle.

READ

Read the passage slowly and carefully, attentive to the details.

THINK

Although this anecdote may not be immediately applicable to the specific circumstances of your life, consider why it was included in the Scriptures. Does "But Moses' hands got tired" seem to be a bit of an understatement? Perhaps God sometimes assigns tasks that actually cannot be completed on our own. Although perseverance and determination to follow Jesus are essential, so are good friends. Who is in your life, holding up your tired hands? How can you do the same for them?

PRAY

Specifically thank God in writing for friends who have stood beside you in the past to help you complete superhuman tasks. Lift up those whom you are trying to support or needing to support in such a way in the future.

LIVE

God makes some tasks an opportunity to reflect on humility and on unity. Whatever your task today, look to the people who are supporting you in it and express gratitude rather than assuming you're standing all on your own.

EYES WIDE OPEN IN GRATITUDE

COLOSSIANS 4:2-6

2-4   Pray diligently. Stay alert, with your eyes wide open in gratitude. Don't forget to pray for us, that God will open doors for telling the mystery of Christ, even while I'm locked up in this jail. Pray that every time I open my mouth I'll be able to make Christ plain as day to them.

5-6   Use your heads as you live and work among outsiders. Don't miss a trick. Make the most of every opportunity. Be gracious in your speech. The goal is to bring out the best in others in a conversation, not put them down, not cut them out.

READ

Read this short passage with full attention. Each phrase is packed with significance.

THINK

Reflect on someone you consider gracious. What does that mean exactly? What does it mean to be gracious in your speech? As women, we love to talk — especially with our friends. Does your conversation with your friends bring out the best in others? What is the focus of your conversation? Do you idolize your own witty banter more than bringing about fruitful discussion? How about how you discuss others? How is speech particularly important in "telling the mystery of Christ" to others?

PRAY

Spend some time laying your conversations before the Lord. Be honest and unflinching about your great temptations in speech — whether vocabulary, tone, or topic. Ask the Spirit to guide you toward graciousness.

LIVE

Journal a short list of two or three things you want to have in mind before starting a conversation and after finishing one. Intentionality can do wonders. What do you want a conversation to accomplish? Lay it before God to bless your efforts.

_____

_____

_____

THE JOY OF HEALING

ACTS 3:6-10

6-8   Peter said, "I don't have a nickel to my name, but what I do have, I give you: In the name of Jesus Christ of Nazareth, walk!" He grabbed him by the right hand and pulled him up. In an instant his feet and ankles became firm. He jumped to his feet and walked.

8-10   The man went into the Temple with them, walking back and forth, dancing and praising God. Everybody there saw him walking around and praising God. They recognized him as the one who sat begging at the Temple's Gate Beautiful and rubbed their eyes, astonished, scarcely believing what they were seeing.

READ

As you read this passage, try to approach the idea of healing afresh. Imagine the different responses of the various characters in this account.

THINK

It seems sometimes like dramatic healings are a thing of the ancient times, only written about in the pages of Scripture. The truth is, though, *you* have been healed by the name of Jesus — brought out of just as much spiritual desperation and deformity as the crippled beggar at the gate. Does your response to salvation look like his? Does joy mark your transformed life? Are others able to see the ecstatic praise that separates you from your former identity?

PRAY

Before God, confess the things that keep you from leaping and jumping for joy at your own healed heart and mind. Record the things that God has done for you, and praise him for providing all that you need.

LIVE

Be a woman defined by *joy*. There is never a shortage of big things that God is doing through the name of Jesus in your life. Celebrate your healed heart.

BUILD ON WHAT YOU'VE BEEN GIVEN

2 PETER 1:5-8

5-8   So don't lose a minute in building on what you've been given, complementing your basic faith with good character, spiritual understanding, alert discipline, passionate patience, reverent wonder, warm friendliness, and generous love, each dimension fitting into and developing the others. With these qualities active and growing in your lives, no grass will grow under your feet, no day will pass without its reward as you mature in your experience of our Master Jesus.

READ

Read the passage slowly and carefully.

THINK

This seems like quite an intimidating list, especially when the average American woman is already drowning in her to-do list. However, the key to these qualities is that they are all "building on what you've been given." The Holy Spirit, given to all believers, already has given you all of these gifts and abilities. It is up to you to "own" these things you have been provided with. How can you keep the attitudes listed here from becoming a spiritual "chore"?

PRAY

Thank God for pouring the foundation of your faith—for doing the mighty work of salvation that you could not. Ask God for discernment in how best to "build" on what he has already done. Confess that you cannot do it on your own—ask for specific instructions and guidance on the "where next."

LIVE

Pick one of these qualities and journal a definition in your own words. Write about how you would like to see it develop in your own life, and compare and contrast it to other spiritual characteristics you have meditated on before.

_____

_____

_____

HE IS LISTENING

1 JOHN 5:11-15

11-12   This is the testimony in essence: God gave us eternal life; the life is in his Son. So, whoever has the Son, has life; whoever rejects the Son, rejects life.

13-15   My purpose in writing is simply this: that you who believe in God's Son will know beyond the shadow of a doubt that you have eternal life, the reality and not the illusion. And how bold and free we then become in his presence, freely asking according to his will, sure that he's listening. And if we're confident that he's listening, we know that what we've asked for is as good as ours.

READ

Read this passage carefully, attentively, and observantly. What details catch your eye?

THINK

As women, we possess an especially strong desire to communicate; to be heard is to be safe. How many times have you simply "shut off" your heart because you knew your voice was useless? How many of your insecurities, even the hidden ones, come from someone telling you that no one heard what you had to say? Although God is not our therapist nor our yes-man — not paid or purposed to make us feel "good" about our voice — God does hear us. We're sure that he is listening. How does that give you freedom? What does it mean to be truly "heard" by someone? How can being "heard" by God give you greater confidence?

PRAY

God is listening to you, hearing you, and he has fulfilled all of his promises. Speak to him freely, asking according to his will in confidence.

LIVE

If God truly hears and therefore gives freedom and confidence, then being an imitator of God means listening as he has listened. Journal about those around you who might need the freedom to speak and the confidence that comes from being heard.

_____

_____

_____

DELEGATE

EXODUS 18:17-21,23

17-23   Moses' father-in-law said, "This is no way to go about it. You'll burn out, and the people right along with you. This is way too much for you — you can't do this alone. Now listen to me. Let me tell you how to do this so that God will be in this with you. Be there for the people before God, but let the matters of concern be presented to God. Your job is to teach them the rules and instructions, to show them how to live, what to do. And then you need to keep a sharp eye out for competent men — men who fear God, men of integrity, men who are incorruptible — and appoint them as leaders over groups organized by the thousand, by the hundred, by fifty, and by ten. . . . If you handle the work this way, you'll have the strength to carry out whatever God commands you, and the people in their settings will flourish also."

READ

Set aside any preconceived images you have of Moses before you read this passage. Try to understand the problem Jethro is addressing.

THINK

You might think a lot about Moses the mighty leader (and even the reluctant leader), but it's hard to imagine Moses the overworked. If there is an epidemic in our culture, specifically with women, it is burnout and exhaustion. Perhaps women are especially subject to overwork because their leadership roles in the church and in the home might not be as pronounced or as obvious as those of men. Do you sometimes feel like you have people and tasks lined up in front of you? Jethro's advice is sound, godly wisdom in any circumstance: You're not supposed to do it all alone. Doing that pridefully assumes that you're the only one able to do the appointed task. Ask people you trust for help—not because you're weak or lazy, but simply because by conserving your energy, you will be able to serve God better than if you are stretched thin.

PRAY

Thank God for good people who counsel you against overwork. Thank God for the good creation of rest, and spend some time confessing the habits that keep you from balancing work and rest successfully. Ask for wisdom and discernment in how to best keep burnout at bay and trust more in God than your own ability.

LIVE

Journal reflectively about rest and work in your life. What are the nonessentials? What are the essentials that can be divided more evenly? Who do you need to ask for help and why? Consider that asking for help might actually bless and not burden others.

HE HAD YOU IN MIND

EPHESIANS 1:3-6

3-6 How blessed is God! And what a blessing he is! He's the Father of our Master, Jesus Christ, and takes us to the high places of blessing in him. Long before he laid down earth's foundations, he had us in mind, had settled on us as the focus of his love, to be made whole and holy by his love. Long, long ago he decided to adopt us into his family through Jesus Christ. (What pleasure he took in planning this!) He wanted us to enter into the celebration of his lavish gift-giving by the hand of his beloved Son.

READ

Read this passage, allowing Paul's enthusiasm to infect you. Engage with his excitement as you read.

THINK

Recall a time that you have felt loved and cherished. God's love multiplies that by far. Long before you even existed, before the world was formed, God had *you* in mind. No romance or devotion could possibly match his depth of care for you. Women in this world often feel valued or rejected based on who is in relationship with them. We often assume that we are deeply flawed when relationships do not come together. However, God knew your flaws and yet pursued you, came after you, and made you a part of his family forever.

PRAY

Paul describes God's love being directed toward us before the foundation of the earth was laid. Journal another prayer of praise describing the love of God, especially as it compares in magnitude to human love you have known. Don't be somber—respond with joy as Paul did.

_____

_____

_____

LIVE

The best thing about God's enduring love is that it goes before you and beyond you—it swallows up all of your failures and fears and grafts you into the generous party that he is throwing for all of creation. Find ways to express your joy over this in the midst of all your comings and goings today.

LEAPING AND DANCING BEFORE GOD

2 SAMUEL 6:12-16

12-16   It was reported to King David that GOD had prospered Obed-Edom and his entire household because of the Chest of God. So David thought, "I'll get that blessing for myself," and went and brought up the Chest of God from the house of Obed-Edom to the City of David, celebrating extravagantly all the way, with frequent sacrifices of choice bulls. David, ceremoniously dressed in priest's linen, danced with great abandon before GOD. The whole country was with him as he accompanied the Chest of GOD with shouts and trumpet blasts. But as the Chest of GOD came into the City of David, Michal, Saul's daughter, happened to be looking out a window. When she saw King David leaping and dancing before GOD, her heart filled with scorn.

READ

Read the passage slowly and carefully, focusing especially on the last verse about David's wife Michal.

THINK

In the midst of this scene of incredible joy, Michal is looking on her husband's "antics" with scorn. It might be easy to judge her as a party pooper, but the text later reveals that David was essentially dancing in his underwear. Clearly dignity was not high on his priority list, but it was important to Michal — perhaps too important. Do you ever find yourself overly concerned with the "indignity" of others? Where do you see it lurking in your own heart? How can you be a woman who joins and promotes the joy of others instead of judging and regulating it?

PRAY

Confess to God the scorn that might be in the corners of your heart. Ask the Holy Spirit to root out the bad attitudes at the heart of that response. Ask God for a new heart of confident, pure joy — a heart that not only refuses to judge the joy of others, but in fact joins in the rejoicing. Pray for a spirit that is unafraid to dance and ignores the opinions of others.

LIVE

Journal about the ways in which you can join others' joy instead of judging it. Shame has no place in the kingdom.

_____

_____

_____

RESCUED FROM DARK DUNGEONS

COLOSSIANS 1:10-14

10-12 As you learn more and more how God works, you will learn how to do *your* work. We pray that you'll have the strength to stick it out over the long haul — not the grim strength of gritting your teeth but the glory-strength God gives. It is strength that endures the unendurable and spills over into joy, thanking the Father who makes us strong enough to take part in everything bright and beautiful that he has for us.

13-14 God rescued us from dead-end alleys and dark dungeons. He's set us up in the kingdom of the Son he loves so much, the Son who got us out of the pit we were in, got rid of the sins we were doomed to keep repeating.

READ

Read the passage slowly and carefully, visualizing the imagery.

THINK

In the life of a Christian, where you are surrounded by "good" things, it might be hard to visualize sin as such a powerful and dark force. But it was. You were not simply a little down on your luck before Jesus. You were in darkness, in prison, doomed to keep up a hopeless cycle. Journal about some of the pits and endless cycles God rescued you from.

_____

_____

_____

PRAY

Praise God for the specific dungeons he has released you from. Confess the cycles of sin that still seem to suck you in. Ask for a full revelation and understanding of the ways in which God has transported you into his kingdom so that you can live in "glory-strength" and not your own "gritting your teeth" strength.

LIVE

You are no longer in the midst of dead-end alleys and dark dungeons. Let your life today reflect that God has set you up "in the kingdom of the Son he loves so much" so that you can "take part in everything bright and beautiful."

TAKING GOD'S NAME

PSALM 33:18-22

18-19   Watch this: God's eye is on those who respect him,
        the ones who are looking for his love.
    He's ready to come to their rescue in bad times;
        in lean times he keeps body and soul together.

20-22   We're depending on God;
        he's everything we need.
    What's more, our hearts brim with joy
        since we've taken for our own his holy name.
    Love us, God, with all you've got —
        that's what we're depending on.

READ

Read the simple words of this psalm slowly and carefully, meditating in depth on the meaning of each phrase.

THINK

What does it mean to take someone's name? Even if you are unmarried, you know other women who have literally and legally left some of their identity behind to share in a new one. Taking God's holy name, however, is not about leaving a part of yourself behind. It actually means gaining your truest identity as a beloved bride of Christ. God is giving you a share of his abundance and his very kingdom; he has given you absolutely everything you need. How do you think God expects you to respond to taking on his holy name?

PRAY

Praise and thank God for giving you his own holy name. Ask for a sense of what it means to assume his identity and to be completely dependent on him. Pray for the Spirit to increase your satisfaction in all that he provides, even in the midst of lean times.

LIVE

Journal about how God has demonstrated to you that he has given his own name for you to take on. What do you imagine when you think of that concept, and what is the impact on your daily life?

_____

_____

_____

FRIENDSHIP WITH GOD

ROMANS 5:9-11

9-11   Now that we are set right with God by means of this sacrificial death, the consummate blood sacrifice, there is no longer a question of being at odds with God in any way. If, when we were at our worst, we were put on friendly terms with God by the sacrificial death of his Son, now that we're at our best, just think of how our lives will expand and deepen by means of his resurrection life! Now that we have actually received this amazing friendship with God, we are no longer content to simply say it in plodding prose. We sing and shout our praises to God through Jesus, the Messiah!

READ

Read the passage slowly aloud to yourself. Try not to tune out familiar ideas. Tune in and be attentive to the language.

THINK

As women especially, our friends influence our lives deeply. You laugh with them, talk with them for hours, seek them for counsel, and love to simply experience life alongside of them. Friends are a safe place for self-discovery, where you don't have to worry about whether or not you are wearing makeup or are otherwise "put together." Consider Paul's word choice in this passage. He does not talk about an "understanding" with God in which God simply puts up with us — but he talks about "friendship with God." There is no question of distance or desperation — Jesus' death has brought you near and given you a companionship that cannot be shaken. Does that thought fill you with as much joy and ecstasy as it does for Paul? Or have you forgotten and pushed that concept to the corner of your mind? How does it change the way you live?

PRAY

Praise God for the gospel — for the sacrifice of his Son in order to bring *you* near. Ask God for a renewed sense of wonder at this familiar truth. Ask God for a sense of friendship with him, a depth of relationship that helps you to move beyond the concept of a distant Creator off in the sky and instead brings you a sense of nearness. Thank God for this incredible truth.

LIVE

Determine to overcome whatever it is that prevents you from sensing closeness with God. Today, allow yourself to indulge in the joy of friendship with the Almighty.

GLORY JUST AROUND THE CORNER

1 PETER 4:12-16

12-13 Friends, when life gets really difficult, don't jump to the conclusion that God isn't on the job. Instead, be glad that you are in the very thick of what Christ experienced. This is a spiritual refining process, with glory just around the corner.

14-16 If you're abused because of Christ, count yourself fortunate. It's the Spirit of God and his glory in you that brought you to the notice of others. If they're on you because you broke the law or disturbed the peace, that's a different matter. But if it's because you're a Christian, don't give it a second thought. Be proud of the distinguished status reflected in that name!

READ

Read this passage through slowly. Relish every word.

THINK

Have you ever felt like your life was completely out of control? Whether from deep pain or simply the all-too-normal chaos of your daily tasks, it is tempting to assume that God is not doing what he "should" when things are difficult. Peter's solution, however, is not to simply wait until the hard things are over, trying to survive — but instead to be glad. Difficulty, complexity, longing, even weariness were all made holy by Jesus as he walked through this earth. It is part of the process of living the Christian life and in fact makes us more like Christ than comfort would.

PRAY

Confess to the Father if you have been doubtful (in thought or in practice) of his supreme reign over all things. Be honest with him about the difficulties in your life and your struggle to trust in the best possible outcome. Ask God for the eyes to see a refining work in your life and the hope to believe that glory is "just around the corner."

LIVE

Why does suffering align us more closely to Christ? Journal about the ways in which difficulty can bring about a more Jesus-like attitude.

_____

_____

_____

JOY LIKE A RIVER

JOHN 16:22-24

22-23   When I see you again, you'll be full of joy, and it will be a joy no one can rob from you. You'll no longer be so full of questions.

23-24   This is what I want you to do: Ask the Father for whatever is in keeping with the things I've revealed to you. Ask in my name, according to my will, and he'll most certainly give it to you. Your joy will be a river overflowing its banks!

READ

Read these words of Jesus to his disciples. Imagine how they might have felt. Read the passage again, slowly, allowing it to speak directly to you.

THINK

Have you ever waited eagerly for someone to appear after a long separation? Joy swallows up the occasion. Of course there are questions — about the trip, about the time you spent apart — but for a few moments you are simply suspended in absolute glee at their presence. Jesus promises this joy to his disciples — the joy that comes from a resurrected and ever-present Savior, who leaves his Spirit with us always. More importantly, Jesus promises this is a joy that cannot be taken away. What forces, internal and external, threaten to take your joy at the presence of Jesus in your life? What does it mean that your joy cannot be taken away once it is given?

PRAY

Do as Jesus commands and ask all your heart desires within God's will. Lay out before God all of the things that keep you from experiencing joy. Ask God for guidance if some of the joy-killing habits need to be changed, and ask for the direction that will lead you to the fullest sense of his unchanging gifts. God provides — and what he gives cannot be taken away.

LIVE

Your joy cannot be taken from you, which means no matter what circumstances, your joy should be a constant source of comfort. Journal about the things that keep you from joy and the ways in which Jesus' presence is stronger.

_____

_____

_____

LOOK FOR THE BEST IN EACH OTHER

1 THESSALONIANS 5:13-15

13-15 Get along among yourselves, each of you doing your part. Our counsel is that you warn the freeloaders to get a move on. Gently encourage the stragglers, and reach out for the exhausted, pulling them to their feet. Be patient with each person, attentive to individual needs. And be careful that when you get on each other's nerves you don't snap at each other. Look for the best in each other, and always do your best to bring it out.

READ

Read the passage slowly and carefully, pausing to consider how each phrase links to the next.

THINK

Journal about a specific person in your life who either demonstrates this to you or whom you need to approach with this demeanor. Apply this specifically with some meditation on how God would want you to act on these commands.

_____

_____

_____

PRAY

You cannot act out any kindness without Jesus working in your heart and modeling generosity for you. Ask God for a deeper and fuller sense of his grace, which is the root of all good relationships. Pray for the courage to be selfless but not spineless. Ask for genuine kindness, not just a "nice" mask. Pray over your relationships.

LIVE

In relating to others, the key is humility. Remember that at any given time you have been or might be a straggler, the exhausted and the needy. Reach out to others as God reached out to you.

GOD'S CONTAINER

2 TIMOTHY 2:20-21

20-21 In a well-furnished kitchen there are not only crystal goblets and silver platters, but waste cans and compost buckets — some containers used to serve fine meals, others to take out the garbage. Become the kind of container God can use to present any and every kind of gift to his guests for their blessing.

READ

Read the passage slowly aloud, imagining the visual as you go.

THINK

Paul gives us an easy image to help us remember our place in God's household. We are vessels. It is not really about you — your own beauty or form or shape. Instead, what is important is what is poured into you by God the Father. You do not exist for yourself, but instead to be a "container" for "every kind of gift" to God's guests, meaning those he loves. What do you think God fills you with as his vessel? How can you put yourself in such a position of service to God on a daily basis?

PRAY

Thank God for filling you with good things. Ask to be "emptied" of the stuff that isn't necessary for serving his purposes. Ask for discernment in how to serve God's guests around you in your community.

LIVE

Journal about the sort of things that you want to "contain" for God's guests. By God's grace, seek to become the kind of container he can use to deliver those things to all you encounter today.

_____

_____

_____

THE GOD OF GREEN HOPE

ROMANS 15:13

13 Oh! May the God of green hope fill you up with joy, fill you up with peace, so that your believing lives, filled with the life-giving energy of the Holy Spirit, will brim over with hope!

READ

Read this blessing with appropriate expression. Read it aloud several times and try to catch Paul's contagious joy.

THINK

When you converse with Christian women about the Spirit, you might often talk about discernment, wisdom, endurance, strength, and other serious topics. But how often are you discussing the God of hope? The Spirit is abundant, causing peace and joy to crop up like the green grass in spring. How often do you pray for the joy of others, a sense of the life-giving energy of the Holy Spirit? How often are you focused on just "making it through" instead of abundant, overflowing peace?

PRAY

Write out your own prayer of both thanksgiving and supplication, focusing on the word "hope," "peace," or "joy."

_____

_____

_____

LIVE

God is a God of hope, joy, and peace. Don't get so stuck in the "serious" stuff of faith that you miss the sheer bliss of God's presence.

MORE THAN ENOUGH

PSALM 4:6-8

6-7 Why is everyone hungry for *more*? "More, more," they say.
"More, more."
I have God's more-than-enough,
More joy in one ordinary day

7-8 Than they get in all their shopping sprees.
At day's end I'm ready for sound sleep,
For you, GOD, have put my life back together.

READ

Read this psalm attentively, focusing on the repetition and the imagery. Repeat the last five lines several times over.

THINK

Though you might run with good Christian folks who are hardly out to spend Daddy's credit card, materialism is still a rampant and often overlooked plague in the church. Write reflectively about the "more, more" that you sense as a woman in our culture and the way God's "more-than-enough" can help.

_____

_____

_____

PRAY

Confess to God the desire for "more" that eats away at you — whether in the form of materialism or simply refusing to be satisfied with all he has already graciously given. Ask for a heart of contentment and the eyes to recognize the great gift of grace. Pray for the peace that comes from trusting in God alone.

LIVE

The unending desire for "more" apart from God will only end in sleepless nights and unsatisfied anxieties. God has put your life back together — redeemed you from the grave itself. What more could you possibly need? Live today with the attitude that you have already been given everything.

A LIFETIME OF LOVE

PSALM 30:4-5

4-5   All you saints! Sing your hearts out to God!
        Thank him to his face!
He gets angry once in a while, but across
        a lifetime there is only love.
The nights of crying your eyes out
        give way to days of laughter.

READ

Read the words of this psalm aloud, slowly and carefully. Try to feel the emotions of the psalmist as you read.

THINK

God is a God of transformation — a God who is changeless but who brings about great and beautiful change. His love is constant, spanning across a lifetime. But of all of the things that remain, grief and sorrow are not on the list. They don't last. Because of God, those always give way to joyous laughter. What is the response of the psalmist to this? What does he urge his audience to do?

PRAY

Thank God "to his face"! Praise him for all of the times his love has remained unchanging, even when you have strayed far away. Thank him for forgiveness. Thank him for transforming your grief and your loss into enduring growth and new, unexpected joys. See how long you can sustain your gratitude for the good God has done.

LIVE

Let the truth of a God who changes grief into joy guide you. Remember that what seems like an eternity of pain or difficulty will always turn into something good God is making. Don't ever stop singing your heart out to God!

JUBILATION HEARD FAR AND WIDE

NEHEMIAH 12:27-29,43

27-29   When it came time for the dedication of the wall, they tracked down and brought in the Levites from all their homes in Jerusalem to carry out the dedication exuberantly: thanksgiving hymns, songs, cymbals, harps, and lutes. The singers assembled from all around Jerusalem, from the villages of the Netophathites, from Beth Gilgal, from the farms at Geba and Azmaveth — the singers had built villages for themselves all around Jerusalem. . . .

43   That day they offered great sacrifices, an exuberant celebration because God had filled them with great joy. The women and children raised their happy voices with all the rest. Jerusalem's jubilation was heard far and wide.

READ

Read this passage about the rebuilding and rededication of Jerusalem with careful attention to the tone. Don't get lost in the foreign names — focus on what is occurring and picture the occasion.

THINK

Did you notice that the singers actually camped out around the walls of Jerusalem? They took their task of celebration seriously. Their praise wasn't just a passing part of the service or a snatch of thought in the morning — it was for a certain time in their lives a completely life-altering experience. Jerusalem's shouts of praise were "heard far and wide." Life in the new covenant means that our communities are mixed. We don't praise as an entire nation or as an entire group of workers, but when we assemble on Sunday morning. Nevertheless, you can be a woman committed to making praise a cornerstone of whatever community you find yourself in. How can you make praise heard throughout the world, even if it is not literal choral singing?

PRAY

Confess to God the ways you have put praise and thanksgiving on the back shelf. Ask for wisdom and strength in making praise central to your life, to the point that you will "relocate" to make it a priority. Practice the first step by praising all that God has rebuilt in your own life and community.

LIVE

Journal about some ways that you intend to seriously commit to praise and joy. How can you help shape the community you're in to that end as well?

THIS IS YOUR FATHER YOU'RE DEALING WITH

MATTHEW 6:7-8,14-15

7-8 The world is full of so-called prayer warriors who are prayer-ignorant. They're full of formulas and programs and advice, peddling techniques for getting what you want from God. Don't fall for that nonsense. This is your Father you are dealing with, and he knows better than you what you need. . . .

14-15 In prayer there is a connection between what God does and what you do. You can't get forgiveness from God, for instance, without also forgiving others. If you refuse to do your part, you cut yourself off from God's part.

READ

Read the words of Jesus here slowly and carefully, pausing to consider their full meaning.

THINK

This passage is pretty straightforward. We cannot ask from God without expecting that we need to return what he gives. If he is gracious to forgive, not holding grudges or standing on grievances, how can you say you truly receive his Spirit if you do not do the same thing? We often think of forgiveness in terms of a big, dramatic act for an obvious dramatic act of wrongdoing. But is forgiveness a more subtle and more constant need in your life and relationships? Do you have grudges you are not even fully aware of?

PRAY

Ask God to uncover the lack of forgiveness in your heart. Inquire after the Spirit's discernment in the relationships that need mending and the old sins that need letting go. Ask God to teach you forgiveness like his, which comes from an overflow of love and grace and doesn't need to hold on to wrongs of the past.

LIVE

Journal about forgiveness. If you don't have any large or long-standing grudges, what do you think forgiveness translates to in your ordinary life and daily interactions? What greater level of forgiveness do you need God to teach you? How can you put that forgiveness into action today? Does it include forgiving yourself?

_____

_____

_____

THE NEW PLAN

HEBREWS 10:12-18

12-18   As a priest, Christ made a single sacrifice for sins, and that was it! Then he sat down right beside God and waited for his enemies to cave in. It was a perfect sacrifice by a perfect person to perfect some very imperfect people. By that single offering, he did everything that needed to be done for everyone who takes part in the purifying process. The Holy Spirit confirms this:

> This new plan I'm making with Israel
>> isn't going to be written on paper,
>> isn't going to be chiseled in stone;
> This time "I'm writing out the plan *in* them,
>> carving it on the lining of their hearts."

He concludes,

> I'll forever wipe the slate clean of their sins.

Once sins are taken care of for good, there's no longer any need to offer sacrifices for them.

READ

Read the passage slowly and carefully.

THINK

Though you don't make literal sacrifices for sin in a temple, you might still be tempted to do obsessive penance for sins that are long past. Do guilt and shame still chase you sometimes? "Grace alone" is a concept that is very easy to say and very hard to believe deeply. The important part of this passage is in pointing out the finality of Christ's sacrifice and the way that God identifies you as a result of it. Not only has he wiped out your sin, he has written his plan for creation and the kingdom on *your* heart! Would God choose an unfit place to put his plans?

PRAY

Confess to God the old sins that seem to haunt you or have so much hold in your life. Be honest about what drives you to want to keep "addressing" them, and ask for increased faith and hope in the sufficiency of Jesus' sacrifice.

LIVE

Today, live in the confidence that God has perfected you and that his plan for you is perfect.

WORDS, WORDS, WORDS

MATTHEW 12:34-37

34-37 You have minds like a snake pit! How do you suppose what you say is worth anything when you are so foul-minded? It's your heart, not the dictionary, that gives meaning to your words. A good person produces good deeds and words season after season. An evil person is a blight on the orchard. Let me tell you something: Every one of these careless words is going to come back to haunt you. There will be a time of Reckoning. Words are powerful; take them seriously. Words can be your salvation. Words can also be your damnation.

READ

Read this passage slowly and carefully, considering the full weight of Jesus' words. As he suggests, take them seriously.

THINK

Simply stated, women tend to use more words and enter into many more conversations than our male counterparts. Because they are even more common, however, they should be used with even more caution and thoughtfulness — with thought behind each one. Journal about an experience that has revealed to you how serious words can be — whether it was your words or the words of others. Was it saving or condemning, and what effects did it have?

_____

_____

_____

PRAY

Confess to God your useless and idle words. Words that are thoughtless or words that are intended to harm are poisonous. Pray for the discernment to use words as a force of powerful redemption and incredible service to others. Ask for the difficult work of thinking before speaking and for the way you can encourage other women around you to be women of wise words.

LIVE

Today, use careful words to encourage and build up. Avoid environments and resist emotional states that tempt you to produce useless, careless words.

A WELL-TAUGHT TONGUE

ISAIAH 50:4

4   The Master, God, has given me
     a well-taught tongue,
So I know how to encourage tired people.
     He wakes me up in the morning,
Wakes me up, opens my ears
     to listen as one ready to take orders.

READ

Read this passage slowly and carefully, pausing after each phrase.

THINK

This passage is from the perspective of the "Servant of God" described extensively throughout Isaiah. This Servant is often considered a prophecy of the roles that Christ would fulfill. However, you follow in the Servant's footsteps as a follower of God. What he does, you should do. What do you think it means that God gives his servants a "well-taught tongue"? What has he given you specifically that is comparable? Could it be skillful words, good intuition, the format or setting in which to speak to many people at once or to a few people deeply and personally? For what purpose does God want you as a servant to use that gift? Though you might be one of the tired people yourself, consider that Jesus, the Servant, uses his words to encourage *you* so that you can in turn encourage others. Encouraging others never takes away from your precious store of energy.

PRAY

Ask God for specific guidance on the use of your "well-taught tongue." Thank him for providing you with the gifts and the means to speak encouragement. Pray for discernment on who in your life is in need of ministry, great and small. Ask for the courage to "wake up" and take instructions and the endurance to follow through.

LIVE

Consider one person you will encounter in your life today who is tired and in need of encouragement. Get creative and find a way to encourage them and lift them up.

BIGHEARTED AND COURTEOUS

TITUS 3:1-8

1-2 Remind the people to respect the government and be law-abiding, always ready to lend a helping hand. No insults, no fights. God's people should be bighearted and courteous.

3-8 It wasn't so long ago that we ourselves were stupid and stubborn, dupes of sin, ordered every which way by our glands, going around with a chip on our shoulder, hated and hating back. But when God, our kind and loving Savior God, stepped in, he saved us from all that. It was all his doing; we had nothing to do with it. He gave us a good bath, and we came out of it new people, washed inside and out by the Holy Spirit. Our Savior Jesus poured out new life so generously. God's gift has restored our relationship with him and given us back our lives. And there's more life to come — an eternity of life! You can count on this.

READ

Pick out three or four of the key words in this passage and attempt to define them in your own words. Then, reread the passage slowly and carefully, going into more thoughtful depth.

_____

_____

_____

THINK

More than ever, conversations and opinions about government permeate the culture. Whether in person or in social media, everyone has a cutting comment, a crying fear, or a condemnation for the people in charge. Governments fight and solicit for the "women's vote" and women's issues are a hot-button topic, eliciting far more emotional response and hysteria than any issue alone could. While these things are certainly important, you must remember that God has not lost control of the universe or allowed any ruler or rulers to slip by. He is in charge, and he does not _need_ government alone to achieve his rule and his purposes. In fact, what he asks of you is bigheartedness and respect that is not conditional. He certainly doesn't need or want your insults or fights.

PRAY

Pray to rise to this high standard of Christian mercy and generosity in all of your conversations. Ask for God to increase the size of your heart and your courteousness, especially as you discuss the government and those in authority with your friends, family, and even your spouse. Spend time praying for your government — it will force you to remember that government consists of people made in God's image.

LIVE

Your service is more valuable to God's purposes than your self-serving or clever rebellion. Your prayers mean more than your careless comments. You are called to be courteous in person and in conversation about your leaders. Don't seek to glorify your own opinions — instead follow the love of Jesus.

YOU ARE AN ORIGINAL

GALATIANS 5:25-26

25-26 Since this is the kind of life we have chosen, the life of the Spirit, let us make sure that we do not just hold it as an idea in our heads or a sentiment in our hearts, but work out its implications in every detail of our lives. That means we will not compare ourselves with each other as if one of us were better and another worse. We have far more interesting things to do with our lives. Each of us is an original.

READ

Read the passage to be encouraged and exhorted.

THINK

In trying to live the life of the Spirit, it is tempting to look around you to see how others measure up — either assuming they are more spiritual or less spiritual and so falling into both depression and pride. Why does Paul say *not* to compare yourself with others? Is comparing yourself with others something that you struggle with? What does that reveal about where you place your trust?

PRAY

Ask God for discernment in the details — the ways you can practically live out your new life in Christ. Confess to God your comparisons to others, or even to some impossible standards in your mind. Ask for the eyes to see the people in your life with God's eyes, without envy or fear. Ask for confidence, trust, and hope in the original work God is doing through you.

LIVE

Write about your envies and insecurities. Reexamine them through the light of the cross. Write about some of the differences in your personality and gifting that may have led to that experience.

_____

_____

_____

GOD-TALK AND GOD-ACTS

JAMES 2:14-17

14-17 Dear friends, do you think you'll get anywhere in this if you learn all the right words but never do anything? Does merely talking about faith indicate that a person really has it? For instance, you come upon an old friend dressed in rags and half-starved and say, "Good morning, friend! Be clothed in Christ! Be filled with the Holy Spirit!" and walk off without providing so much as a coat or a cup of soup — where does that get you? Isn't it obvious that God-talk without God-acts is outrageous nonsense?

READ

Read this passage slowly and carefully, dwelling on the strongest key words as you encounter them.

THINK

Think carefully about the image James gives of an old friend in rags left behind. Although most of us are not so obviously callous, is there a way in which you might address spiritual poverty and desperation with unsatisfactory "Christianese"? As women in the church, it is easy and even common to cook a meal or provide a card of encouragement, which are not at all bad things. However, does your heart match your words? Are you willing to simply sit with those who are grieving and listen? Or are you eager to dish out words about God's sovereignty? How can your God-acts increase to strengthen and support your God-talk?

PRAY

Write a prayer of confession for the places and the people in which your God-acts have not matched your God-words. Pray for ways to put your faithful speech and your Christian catchphrases into real, true, genuine faith and relationships.

_____

_____

_____

LIVE

Often God-acts make you feel accomplished, like you have done something concrete. But God calls you to relationships, not simply acts of service that can be dropped off at the doorstep. Pursue faithful actions in your community, especially with those in any sort of need or trouble.

HE DOESN'T SCRIMP

PSALM 84:10-12

10-12　One day spent in your house, this beautiful place of worship,
　　　beats thousands spent on Greek island beaches.
I'd rather scrub floors in the house of my God
　　　than be honored as a guest in the palace of sin.
All sunshine and sovereign is GOD,
　　　generous in gifts and glory.
He doesn't scrimp with his traveling companions.
　　　It's smooth sailing all the way with GOD-of-the-Angel-Armies.

READ

Read the words of this psalmist. Consider his tone as you read the lines of this poem.

THINK

There is a certain atmosphere that takes over when you are in the presence of someone you love—a grandmother or mother, or simply a mentor who has gone out of their way to bring you into their life. This bedrock truth of the longing for acceptance, to be a part of something bigger and more beautiful than yourself, is the core principle of praise. As a woman, how can you make your home and household a symbol that points to this generosity of God and the belonging that he brings?

PRAY

Write your own praises to God for the things that are better than time apart from God. Come up with your own creative ways to express the things that God's presence surpasses.

_____

_____

_____

LIVE

The psalmist expresses that one day with God is better than a thousand in luxurious leisure. But God's presence is no longer in a temple or a tabernacle—he is among you, present with you. Live your life with the joy of belonging and of abundant worship and praise.

BRIMMING WITH BLESSING

PSALM 23:5-6

5   You serve me a six-course dinner
        right in front of my enemies.
    You revive my drooping head;
        my cup brims with blessing.

6   Your beauty and love chase after me
        every day of my life.
    I'm back home in the house of GOD
        for the rest of my life.

READ

Read the end of this familiar psalm with fresh eyes. Really visualize the images that the poet provides. Place yourself inside of the scene.

THINK

Who is doing the action in this psalm? Note all of the words that are describing God the Good Shepherd's role — he is serving, reviving, and chasing after you. Christianity places a lot of emphasis on the pursuit of God, but the fundamental tenet of our faith is that God pursues *us*. There is also a lot of buzz in Christian culture on men being the pursuers of women in a relationship — but it is vital to remember that God is the original and the source, the one who brings you into his household and serves you with his leadership. How long does this amazing relationship last, according to the psalmist?

PRAY

Praise God for his good shepherding. Thank him for specific blessings, especially the ones present *today,* that make your cup flow over. Praise him for his constant presence and pursuit of you and for his reviving Spirit. Ask for this sense of identity to make you receptive to God's gifts.

LIVE

Reflect on the ways in which God has "served," "revived," or "chased after" you in the past. Use these memories to remind you of God's role of redemption in your life, no matter how hectic your day becomes or how exhausted you feel.

A GOOD KING

ZECHARIAH 9:9-10

9-10   Shout and cheer, Daughter Zion!
     Raise the roof, Daughter Jerusalem!
Your king is coming!
     a good king who makes all things right,
     a humble king riding a donkey,
     a mere colt of a donkey.
I've had it with war — no more chariots in Ephraim,
     no more war horses in Jerusalem,
     no more swords and spears, bows and arrows.
He will offer peace to the nations,
     a peaceful rule worldwide,
     from the four winds to the seven seas.

READ

Read this prophecy about Jesus with open eyes, attentive to the detail and the tone of this message for God's people. Read the passage slowly several times.

THINK

What is the "war" you are pressured into in your daily life? What are the roles that you are tempted to pursue because of pride and image? What leadership roles are you in?

PRAY

Ask God for the humility modeled by the King of the universe, Jesus Christ. Confess to God the "war horses" that you have taken, pursuing your own glory and position. Pray for the courage to step down and offer humble leadership to show off God's power, might, and forgiveness instead of your own strength. Ask for specific and practical ways to practice humility in your current situation.

LIVE

If anyone had a right to make a grand entrance, it was Jesus. But he chose to enter his city promising peace, humility, and righteousness instead of a display of his own power. Arrange your life to show off God's love and grace, with yourself as a vessel and not the centerpiece of God's glory.

TRUE GREATNESS

MARK 10:41-45

41-45   When the other ten heard of this conversation, they lost their tempers with James and John. Jesus got them together to settle things down. "You've observed how godless rulers throw their weight around," he said, "and when people get a little power how quickly it goes to their heads. It's not going to be that way with you. Whoever wants to be great must become a servant. Whoever wants to be first among you must be your slave. That is what the Son of Man has done: He came to serve, not to be served — and then to give away his life in exchange for many who are held hostage."

READ

Read the passage slowly and carefully, considering the very human tendencies of the disciples. How might they have felt on hearing Jesus' words? How do you feel?

THINK

For much of human history, women hardly had any authority in society. Now more than ever, however, women hold positions of power as frequently as men — in the church, in the workplace, and always, if not more than ever, in the home as mothers, wives, and facilitators of finances. But leadership can be lonely. It can leave you feeling isolated in pride ("no one else does as much as I do") or simply feeling entitled. Service is freedom. Serving others makes leadership not about what you can get or do, but about loving, connecting, and growing those under your authority. Jesus came to this earth, not to throw around his authority, but to highlight the love of the Father by his radical service and unspeakable kindness. How can you follow that example in your own positions of authority, great and small?

PRAY

Confess the times when you have "thrown your weight around" and in some way abused the people you had authority over. Be honest with God about the times that pride and survival instinct got in the way of loving service. Ask God for his spirit of humble service to fill you so that you can imitate the way Jesus led. Pray for the courage to be willing to give of yourself in order to serve others.

LIVE

Write about the ways in which you can "become last" in your positions of authority. How should you use your position to serve?

173

_____

_____

_____

RESURRECTION AND LIFE

JOHN 11:21-27

21-22 Martha said, "Master, if you'd been here, my brother wouldn't have died. Even now, I know that whatever you ask God he will give you."

23 Jesus said, "Your brother will be raised up."

24 Martha replied, "I know that he will be raised up in the resurrection at the end of time."

25-26 "You don't have to wait for the End. I am, right now, Resurrection and Life. The one who believes in me, even though he or she dies, will live. And everyone who lives believing in me does not ultimately die at all. Do you believe this?"

27 "Yes, Master. All along I have believed that you are the Messiah, the Son of God who comes into the world."

READ

Read this story slowly, imagining the emotions of this conversation. Try to picture how it might have taken place — body language, tone, setting. Read the passage through slowly once more, considering how the context adds to the famous passage about the Resurrection.

THINK

What mixture of emotions do you think Mary felt as she beheld Jesus after the death of her brother? She had sent to him for help when Lazarus was sick, and Jesus seems to be showing up too late. Yet Jesus offers a promise — one she thinks is in the distant future. Little does she know that what Jesus is promising is a present promise, beyond all belief, about to take place. Resurrection is the ultimate symbol of triumph over sin and death — which seem like the ultimate undefeated villains. God is not going to let sorrow swallow up your life. He is promising victory and life *now*.

PRAY

Confess to God the things that seem so "dead" you do not want to hope for resurrection. Be honest with God about the conflicting emotions you have — lingering feelings of abandonment about the dark and difficult times of your life. Thank him that he is not only present, but working to redeem and resurrect the darkest things in your life. Ask God for the courage to believe in a present and working resurrection — not only in your life, but in the lives of all believers.

LIVE

Journal about the relationships, attitudes, and circumstances that need resurrection from Jesus in this present moment. Hope that he is present and able to work miracles.

OH, YES!

1 TIMOTHY 1:15-17

15-17   Here's a word you can take to heart and depend on: Jesus Christ came into the world to save sinners. I'm proof — Public Sinner Number One — of someone who could never have made it apart from sheer mercy. And now he shows me off — evidence of his endless patience — to those who are right on the edge of trusting him forever.

> Deep honor and bright glory
> to the King of All Time —
> One God, Immortal, Invisible,
> ever and always. Oh, yes!

READ

Read the passage slowly and carefully, pausing with each new phrase.

THINK

What is the tone of Paul's confession of sin? Note that redemption is not a context — it's not a matter of who was the worst sinner and why. Getting stuck on your old sins, even with the guise of repentance, is not healthy or productive. Paul's only purpose in bringing up his absolute sin is to point out how much it demonstrates God's patience. He ends praising God, not bemoaning his sin. Can you turn your dismay over sin into gratitude over God's redemption? Can you learn to view even your failure as a way to display the power and patience of God?

PRAY

Confess the sin in your life. Move from confession to joy and praise. Ask God for help in viewing even your failures as a way to display his glory, mercy, and love. Pray for help in not getting "stuck" thinking about an old sin life.

LIVE

Journal about a painful failure that taught you even more about God's grace. How can you reframe that memory in order to view God's power as bigger than your failure?

_____

_____

_____

GOD CAN'T BREAK HIS WORD

HEBREWS 6:13-18

13-18 When God made his promise to Abraham, he backed it to the hilt, putting his own reputation on the line. He said, "I promise that I'll bless you with everything I have — bless and bless and bless!" Abraham stuck it out and got everything that had been promised to him. When people make promises, they guarantee them by appeal to some authority above them so that if there is any question that they'll make good on the promise, the authority will back them up. When God wanted to guarantee his promises, he gave his word, a rock-solid guarantee — God *can't* break his word. And because his word cannot change, the promise is likewise unchangeable.

READ

Read this passage slowly and carefully.

THINK

Have you ever had a friend, family member, or authority figure break a promise? Have you ever broken a promise to someone you care about? Is it so easy to speak words without having the sense of their full weight, or what it can mean when we do not follow through. No matter who has broken your heart with their unfulfilled promises, in great ways or small, God is the epitome of consistency. He puts his own name on the line, and he will never let you down. His promises are not vague hopes of what he will do, but promises of what will actually come to pass. What are some of the promises of God that you can cling to?

PRAY

Confess to God the anxieties and trust issues that have influenced your relationship with him. Ask for a sense of true trust that God will follow through on all of his good promises. Invite the Spirit to show you what it means to live in the belief that all of God's Word will be fulfilled.

LIVE

Are you living like God's promises are real? Remind yourself of the things God has promised to all believers and what that means specifically to your life and your emotional state today.

TIRED IN THE WAITING

ROMANS 8:26-28

26-28 Meanwhile, the moment we get tired in the waiting, God's Spirit is right alongside helping us along. If we don't know how or what to pray, it doesn't matter. He does our praying in and for us, making prayer out of our wordless sighs, our aching groans. He knows us far better than we know ourselves, knows our pregnant condition, and keeps us present before God. That's why we can be so sure that every detail in our lives of love for God is worked into something good.

READ

Read this passage slowly and carefully.

THINK

Can you identify with feeling "tired in the waiting"? Sometimes the desire for what you've asked of God is so strong, you don't even have the words to know how to pray. The wonderful thing is that God knows your longings and desires even more than you know them yourself. Your patience is not simply a "wait-and-see" or "grin-and-bear-it" event. You can strive for patience in your life because God is working every single detail in your life into something good. Waiting on him isn't about giving up understanding — it's about a deeper sense of God's richer and fuller time line. Have confidence in patience.

PRAY

Keep praying. Although the Spirit translates our groans, it is a helpful process for you to put your desires into words. Praise God for knowing your desires so intimately and working all things toward your good.

LIVE

God is working out the details of your life better than you could yourself. Be patient and confident in God's purposes, even when you do not know how to pray.

PASSIONATE PATIENCE

ROMANS 5:3-5

3-5   There's more to come: We continue to shout our praise even when we're hemmed in with troubles, because we know how troubles can develop passionate patience in us, and how that patience in turn forges the tempered steel of virtue, keeping us alert for whatever God will do next. In alert expectancy such as this, we're never left feeling shortchanged. Quite the contrary — we can't round up enough containers to hold everything God generously pours into our lives through the Holy Spirit!

READ

Read the passage slowly, focusing on the images Paul presents.

THINK

What verbs does Paul use to characterize the spiritual process happening inside the believer? The images are of strength and courage; active things are occurring as a result of trouble. This is not simply about passive endurance. Paul rests all of his hope and faith in the belief that when you feel "hemmed in" — truly without escape — you can still shout praise. What truth does Paul know that allows him to hold such an understanding on the difficulties a believer faces? What is produced from troubles, and how does it make you "alert for whatever God will do next"?

PRAY

Name before God the situations in your life where you feel "hemmed in." Be honest before the Lord about your fears and insecurities, your heartfelt sorrows, and your grief. Come clean if shouting praises seems like the last thing you want to do. Now, praise God for his generosity, starting with what you know — the Cross. Ask God for the eyes to see what is being produced and forged in the midst of that trouble. Thank him for the ways he has shaped you and generously provided for you in past troubles.

LIVE

Practicing is sometimes the only way to get your mind into the habit of thanks, to close the gap between the head and the heart. When you are faced with troubles today, great or small, praise God, silently or aloud, and call to mind his character.

HE COMES ALONGSIDE

2 CORINTHIANS 1:3-5

3-5   All praise to the God and Father of our Master, Jesus the Messiah! Father of all mercy! God of all healing counsel! He comes alongside us when we go through hard times, and before you know it, he brings us alongside someone else who is going through hard times so that we can be there for that person just as God was there for us. We have plenty of hard times that come from following the Messiah, but no more so than the good times of his healing comfort — we get a full measure of that, too.

READ

Read this prayer of thanksgiving, attentive to the details of language and the intent of the author.

THINK

Have you ever felt lonely in your difficult times? Even if you are not fully "through" your difficult circumstances, vulnerable conversation can be a service to you and to those around you. It emphasizes God's glorious capacity as healer rather than your painful self-control. Journal about the ways in which your unique sorrows and circumstances could be used to encourage other women in your community.

_____

_____

_____

PRAY

Pray for God's direction in sharing your difficult stories with others to encourage them. Ask for the courage to go beyond surface words of encouragement and to truly connect with other members of the body, confident that God is working all things for good and has done so already in your past. Praise God for being the Great Healer.

LIVE

Focusing on the way God has brought you through trials is a wonderful spiritual discipline. However, God doesn't deliver you simply for your own good. He has called you into community, and because of God's gospel, your wounds are strengths that contribute to the life of the body. Be bold. Strike up conversation. Be vulnerable.

THIRST FOR LIVING WATER

JOHN 4:7-15

7-8   A woman, a Samaritan, came to draw water. Jesus said, "Would you give me a drink of water?" (His disciples had gone to the village to buy food for lunch.)

9   The Samaritan woman, taken aback, asked, "How come you, a Jew, are asking me, a Samaritan woman, for a drink?" (Jews in those days wouldn't be caught dead talking to Samaritans.)

10   Jesus answered, "If you knew the generosity of God and who I am, you would be asking *me* for a drink, and I would give you fresh, living water."

11-12   The woman said, "Sir, you don't even have a bucket to draw with, and this well is deep. So how are you going to get this 'living water'? Are you a better man than our ancestor Jacob, who dug this well and drank from it, he and his sons and livestock, and passed it down to us?"

13-14   Jesus said, "Everyone who drinks this water will get thirsty again and again. Anyone who drinks the water I give will never thirst — not ever. The water I give will be an artesian spring within, gushing fountains of endless life."

15   The woman said, "Sir, give me this water so I won't ever get thirsty, won't ever have to come back to this well again!"

READ

As you read aloud slowly, visualize this encounter. Imagine the setting and the tone of the conversation.

THINK

Compare Jesus' questions and statements with those of the Samaritan woman. Instead of directly answering her question about Jews and Samaritans, Jesus brings up the "generosity of God" and his own identity. God is *generous*, and he produces water that quenches every thirsty heart. Just what this woman really needs. Do you ever view God's encounters in your life with suspicion? Do you ever grow impatient with spiritual issues, when material issues seem so much more pressing? What is the "thirst" that Jesus is actually referring to, and where do you see it in your own life?

PRAY

Ask Jesus to meet you when and where you least expect him. Confess to him the thirst you feel in your own life — whether it is a familiar brokenness or a longing you cannot even identify. Pause to contemplate the abundant water that Jesus has given to you, and thank him for the places where it has already flowed into your life. Ask for a deeper and greater thirst and a sense of satisfaction in the water of grace.

LIVE

Wherever and whenever you feel a "thirst" that is beyond this world, remember your need has already been met. Remember the generosity of God in all things.

INDEX

Note: Unless denoted by "p.," references are to Day numbers.

ABOUT THE AUTHORS

Eugene H. Peterson is a pastor, scholar, writer, and poet. After teaching at a seminary and then giving nearly thirty years to church ministry in the Baltimore area, he created *The Message*, a vibrant translation of the Bible from the original Greek and Hebrew. Eugene and his wife, Jan, live in his native Montana. They are the parents of three and the grandparents of six.

Michelle Hindman earned her degree in English literature from Westmont College in Santa Barbara, California. In that learning community of faith, she was taught that in pursuing truth, sometimes the questions are just as important as the answers. She has always loved exploring the written word, whether in the pages of fiction or the deep digging of hermeneutics. Because of her passion for good conversation and timeless literature, God has brought her to teach at a classical school in Colorado Springs, Colorado. When she is not grading or writing, Michelle likes to drink tea, hike, and memorize poems.